D0921122

KARMA
CRISIS

Dave —

thanks for giving
these poems
a chance!

Nathan
Brown

3/28/12

MEZCALITA PRESS – Norman, OK

FIRST EDITION, 2012
Copyright © 2012 by Nathan Brown
All Rights Reserved.

ISBN-13: 978-0-9837383-0-5
Library of Congress Control Number: 2012900622

No part of this book may be performed, recorded, or
otherwise transmitted without the written consent of the
author and the permission of the publisher. However,
portions of poems may be cited for book reviews—
favorable or otherwise—without obtaining consent.

Cover Design: Chris Everett
Foam Art: Bess Lovejoy
Back Cover Photo: Rodney Bursiel

MEZCALITA PRESS
Norman, Oklahoma

ALSO BY NATHAN BROWN:
*Letters to the One-Armed Poet: A Memoir of Friendship, Loss,
and Butternut Squash Ravioli* (2011)
My Sideways Heart (2010)
Two Tables Over (2008)
Not Exactly Job (2007)
Suffer the Little Voices (2005)
Ashes Over the Southwest (2005)
Hobson's Choice (2002)

BY NATHAN AND ASHLEY BROWN:
*AGAVE: A Celebration of Tequila in Story, Song, Poetry,
Essay, and Graphic Art*

KARMA
CRISIS

NEW AND SELECTED POEMS

~ Nathan Brown ~

TABLE OF CONTENTS

ACKNOWLEDGEMENTS

Certain pieces from the New Poems chapter first
appeared in these journals and anthologies:

Ain't Nobody That Can Sing Like Me: New Oklahoma Writing
Blood and Thunder: Musings on the Art of Medicine
Chokecherries (at SOMOS, the Society of the Muse of the
Southwest in Taos, New Mexico. Many thanks to
Lorraine Ciancio for quick consideration!)
Concho River Review
Crosstimbers
di-verse-city: Austin International Poetry Festival Anthology
Oklahoma Today Magazine
Sugar Mule
Wichita Falls Literature and Art Review
Windhover
World Literature Today

Thanks to Jim Drummond, Rodney Bursiel, Robert Con
Davis-Undiano, Terri Stubblefield, Billy and Dodee
Crockett, George Economou, and David Gross. Oh...
and The Red Cup, Agora, Flipnotics, The Aztec, and
Caffe Tazza (for ignoring the overdue rent).

A special thanks to Chris Everett, who not only designed
the cover for this book, but for my first three books as
well. Bess Lovejoy, for her fabulous foam etching in that
fabulous looking latte. (You saved us, Bess!) Also, Dr.
Gladys Lewis for publishing—and believing in—my first
three books, in spite of how wet they were behind the
ears.

As always... Mom, Dad, and my daughter Sierra.

                                        ... For Ashley

Karma C r i s i s

new p o e m s

The good news is I know who I am;
that's the bad news, too.

~ Stehpen Dunn

SUCH IS LIFE

The three of them are playing LIFE
when I arrive to pick up my daughter
for our one-day weekend. My ex,
her new hubby, and my little girl

swap orange and green money,
spin the plastic wheel, and move
red, white, and yellow plastic cars
with pink and blue people in them.

My ex constantly checks the rules
on the box lid, as she's always done.

Her husband stares at the floor...
refuses Homeowner's Insurance.

And my baby girl is married,
has a son, and will probably retire
with a few million dollars.

They argue quite a bit over details...
squabble over taxes... and the fact
that my girl chose the ARTIST card.

And I am forced to sit by
and watch
until they are done.

Questions in the Wind

The fists of an Oklahoma wind
pummeled the backs of the gravestones.

But with her thick black ski coat
zipped up all around her, she refused
to give up helping me find
her great-grandparents' names.

I hadn't visited in twelve years...
since we'd buried Grandma Brown.

And my ten-year-old daughter tells me
she's never been in a graveyard before.
So, I asked—"Do you know
what the rectangles of fresh dirt mean?"

She pulls her eyebrows together
and says "Well?" not wanting to say "No."

"It means those graves are new..."

Her eyes blow open in sudden understanding.
She stays closer to me now until we find
who we're looking for. She quietly reads
my face for the story it tells about the strange
cut between death and living on.

Halfway back to the car, I sense
that she's slowed down behind me—
"Dad? Why is this rectangle so small?"

I turn, remain silent, watch the millions
of little calculations in her gray eyes—

watch her grow a few inches
as the answer moves
towards her mouth.

WHITHER IT GOES

Chins slide off palms
in the halls of higher learning,
and the beautiful young grad student
squeaks and stammers her way
through her paper on: *The Universality
of Place in the Poetry of Walt Whitman.*

And the amber waves of her hair
look as if they might drown
in the sea of suggestions
she received from some professor
to put more words like "antinomian"
and "binary" in her presentation.

Such is the hegemonious enterprise
we carry on in the English Buildings
of the post-postmodern world.

And in the hot flush of her cheeks...
and the quivering confusion
of her quaking voice,

the crowd can do little more
than watch her love of poems
begin to die.

Karma Crisis

She glides in the front door
of the all-organic Earth Café
with hairy legs and high heels—

a sweetheart of a hippie chick
who sells Yellow Pages ad slots
to dirty old men behind desks.

She took the job as a stopgap
before the more green-tinted,
planet-saving work she plans to do.

But the fat paycheck she cashes
on Fridays by far surpasses
what her flower-child mind

is able to recycle in the tie-dyed
and environmentally friendly
agendas of her dreams.

And so the revolution rages
in the smoldering factories
of her flickering, hazel eyes.

As the Minister of Propriety
and Fermentation

Mom hands me the list—
    hand-written on the back
    of church stationary—
with a wince of hope in her eyes…

    KJ – 2

is code for a couple of nice
Kendall Jackson Chardonnays.
Vintner's Reserve… her favorite.

Then:
    Champagne
    1 Andre Ex. Dry
    1 Beringer pink…
                   …if enough money

And she handed that list to me
because she is a preacher's wife—
even if that preacher retired years ago.

And this is just how it's done
here on the plains of Oklahoma.

Liberated as she may be,
a temperate, upstanding woman,
married to a Baptist minister,

enlists an accomplice—
    someone beyond redemption—
        to buy her booze.

13 GOIN' ON COUGAR
(To be read in one breath)

Lindsey's awesome boys are the problem 'cept Jessie he's cool. at band practice the other day? anyway we can't ever get anything done. math sucks and I get a C if I don't turn this in tomorrow. *please* dad it's got to be there. and it was just a kiss. he's so shy. I always have to make the first move. oh that's just Ashlee she's just like that. ooo I love this song. turn it back to 104. can we get a burrito? and I'm serious Mr. Jackson only likes Asian students. Jody got caught with pot *and* snow the other day. anyway like I was sayin' boys are the problem I mean the whole freakin' problem omg wtf…

NERUDA'S GARDEN

When the soldiers flooded Neruda's garden
with their orders, that night on Isla Negra,
the poet turned them on their heels
from the top of his stairs
with one careful phrase...

There is only one danger for you here: poetry.

And so it is, I'm reminded,
some poet in the Middle East
lost his hand today, which
makes me sad how safe I am
in America these days.

The worst they would do here?
Tap my phone? Monitor emails?
Or maybe peek at my books,
which worries me very little
when it comes to a politician's
skills with literary interpretation?

Capitol Hill has forgotten this power.
They don't know where to send the soldiers.
They've lost the coordinates for the garden.

But I am at the desk upstairs, writing.
And the garden is here outside my window,
filled with fellow citizens sipping lattes
and driving Toyotas.
                              And I am trying
to become dangerous.

MAKING PAYMENTS

The down payment I handed over
to the receptionist in purple scrubs
makes me grateful for the painkillers
prescribed by my good doctor.

Since the anesthesia allows only
the memory of being wheeled
into the blue and white room filled
with shiny steel and latex gloves,

the knives and blood and needles of it all
stay safely in the world of the imaginary.

So I awake to nothing but a fluffy,
puffy patch of white gauze and tape
as evidence that someone recently
stuck fingers and clamps deep
inside my lower abdomen. That is...

until I first try to move my head
in the recovery room.   Then...

the evidence shoots sharp and clear
throughout pockets and cavities
in my body—places of which
I am normally unaware.

And yet, now, suddenly,
I am quite aware... of the pain...
and the problem that
there is going to be
a balance due.

PHARMACOLOGY REPORT

When we're forced into stillness
by invisible straps and tethers
in a loved-one's eyes, because
they love us… and because
we probably should remain still—
since the nurse strongly suggested it—

we usually wind up on the couch
in the middle of the house,
there with the television
and in good proximity
to the kitchen… where
we're also in plain view
in case we try to escape.

And once there, after a boring while,
we begin to see all the cool projects
we've had in mind—for years now—
for fixing things up around this pit.

And with this peculiar side-effect of surgery,
comes the key benefit of the fantabulous drugs
they send home with us—besides, of course,
killing the synapse-melting pain in the cut—

and that is…
that within about fifteen minutes
we stop thinking about drills, nails,
and paint colors, and begin, simply,
shaping the syllables of words like

    Hydrooo-cooooooo-dooone,

sometimes just howling, softly,
that middle one—cooooooo—

like an arctic wolf
in the frozen air
of the midnight
tundra.

OUT GALLIVANTING

When you live on airplanes
and in cars, crossing rivers
and oceans for months at a time,
home looks at you kinda funny
when you get back to town.

It doesn't want to talk at first.
Instead, it just points out
the disarray of the front yard,
then opens the door to the bathroom
so you can see the little moldy solar systems

that have spun out their designs
all over the toilet. The sink
sputters. The stoic fridge
puts its hands on its hips
and is tapping the floor.

The message is clear.
I hang my head...
keep my mouth shut...
and begin my penance
with Clorox and Lysol.

NATURAL FLAVORS

The trail of their tears
ended—some say—
in Tahlequah, Oklahoma.

But the tears of the remnant
continued to fall long after
their feet came to a stop.

That's how the Cherokee spread
throughout the water supply
of this grassy hinterland...

their salt and blood
seasoning the rose rocks
and dark red dirt.

Under Black Mesa

Whales once swam these prairies,
back when the oceans
used to drink more.

I know this because
I see the black hills
those whales became
when they turned to stone
and sank down to the bottom
of Oklahoma's dusty bed.

WAYFARER

The rocks and cactus
that line Highway 104
of New Mexico's upper east side

rest inside a Paleolithic peace
that my roaming soul
may never know.

The snow-laced scrub brush
of the Canadian Escarpment
demands a silence

that my overworked mouth
and guilt-littered mind
don't know to seek...

while the twitching ears
of the antelope here
in the high desert

continue to hear the song
that no longer vibrates
the worn out bones in my head.

TAMALES AND DIRT
—Santuario de Chimayó, New Mexico

Chimayó sings holy songs
in my ear... a sacred place.

And it's not just Leona's tamales
that inspire my devotion.

It is the hard, back row bench
in the sanctuary that has cradled
the back pockets of innumerable
burning souls, lit up by the torches
life brings to all our little lynchings.

It is the healing dirt
    in the hole
    in the floor
    of the back room
that I've rubbed into these pages
over the last few lost years...

the healing dirt
    in the hole
    in the floor
that the priest replenishes
from a wheelbarrow every night
after the pilgrims leave...

the healing dirt
    in the hole
that I have wiped over
my two tattoos and forehead
so many times now before stepping

back into the sanctuary to pray
that God would deign to lift
the boulders of darkness
off my shrinking mind...

the healing dirt
that has dried hundreds
of my tears, millions
of others'... absorbed them
into its divine drought.

SIDEWINDER HIGHWAY

The rattlesnake of Route 66
slithers and coils under, over,
and all around I-40 in the Southwest.

And in the bright white scorch
of an early summer, its venom
raises blisters on the backs
of New Mexico and Arizona.

Every hundred miles or so,
I'd turn off into one of those towns
like Tucumcari... or Winslow...

just to put a foot on the scaly back
of this crazy road's history.

At the Silver Moon Café
in Santa Rosa, the food is fried
or slathered in red hot chile. Or both.

But I'm still kickin' myself
for passing up gas at $3.87 a gallon
in Kingman, the tail-end of Arizona.

Because, by the time I hit the 118°
of Needles, California, they
were demanding $5.29.

And they know you'll pay it,
there at the front edge of the Devil's
Playground and the Bristol Mountains...

out where the Devil ain't got no gas
in the desert of his obsidian dreams…

out there… where he cooks up
the recipes for all of life's
little disasters.

FELLOW FAILURES

My old Bible sits
in mausoleum silence
on the shelf across the room—

a mossy gravestone
in memory of a good idea.

I walk by sometimes,
lay a flower at its foot
and mourn the genocide
of its millennial wisdom.

I love the stories…
from Noah's alcoholism,
to King David's striptease…

from Paul's long struggle
with bipolar disorder,
to John's suspected substance abuse
in that cell on the Isle of Patmos…

those great men
who helped me believe
that I had something
worth saying
as well.

BIBLICAL PROPORTIONS

When God swings the fist
of weather in Oklahoma,
we pull up seats and lean
into the performance...

here on the stage that gave us
one of the great panoramic visions
of the 20th Century when it comes
to heaven's fits of meteorological rage.

The Dust Bowl—stirred up
by an army of angel wings—
came in like a black tidal wave
of interstellar grit and dirt.

It ground its stained teeth
as it passed over and turned
small homesteads and barns
into dunes and shallow graves.

The few surviving souls
were forced to punch holes
through shingles in the roof
to get a view of the damage.

Heard tell of one old man
who said, *Ol' Noah never
had no troubles like this.
Least he had time to build a boat.*

COTTON-PICKER

He picked cotton as a kid in Cyril
and pushed around cranky milk cows
over on the poor side of the tracks
in a tiny town that didn't have
any wealth on the other side.

After he turned nine, the family moved
across the tracks to what became known
as B & E Street—for Brown & Ellis—
all the postman needed to deliver a letter.

In high school he played shortstop for the Pirates
well enough to get a scholarship to OBU
where, as a lefty, he's held—since '54—
the highest batting average for 55 years.

That was enough at the time
to get the attention of the Oakland A's.
But he became a Baptist preacher instead.

And for the better part of a half century
he tried to teach the better parts of God
to a flock that—more often than not—
acted like a bunch o' cranky milk cows.

And he did what he did
as well as anybody ever has.

And my brothers and I always had skateboards,
warm beds, and hot chocolate in January.

He still gives us what he can—
sometimes more. And I believe
he loves this life and smiles with hands
down deep in secret, sacred pockets,

because he's never forgotten
how those hard dry cotton husks
sliced the hell out of his fingers.

ON THE DESECRATION OF INDEPENDENCE

The Unanimous Declaration of the united Minions in my Mind

WHEN in the Course of human Events, it becomes necessary for a Person to dissolve the Political Illusions which have connected him to the idea that congressmen fighting like 5th graders among the Powers of the Earth, while up there on the Hill, give even the slightest flying flip about the separate and equal Station to which the Laws of Nature and of Nature's God entitle him, as well as them, he must report his loss of all decent Respect for the Opinions of Their Kind, requiring therefore, that he should declare the causes which impel him to the Separation.

HE holds these Truths to be self-evident, but realizes [unlike the Second Continental Congress] that what is self-evident to one, may not be to another [say... for example, Hitler or Gandhi]. Still, it seems to him that all Men are created equal, but that Women and Other Races are as well, and that they are all endowed by their Creator with certain unalienable Rights, that among these are Life, Liberty, and the Pursuit of Happiness [or something like it...say, for instance... Joy]—That to secure these Rights, Governments are instituted among Men and Women, deriving their just Powers from the Consent of the Governed [at least until their Powers and Methods become so exquisitely confusing and obscured that the Governed no longer understand what the hell the Government is doing], that whenever any Form of Government becomes destructive of these Ends, it is the Right of the

People to alter or to abolish it, and to institute new Government [unless, of course, it becomes so entrenched in the mire of its own impenetrable documents and arcana that the People are no longer able to find a way], laying its Foundation on such Principles, and organizing its Powers in such Form, as to them shall seem most likely to effect their Safety and Happiness [since it is, according to the Laws of these States, illegal to take the Members of this Government over into Virginia and collectively hang them all in the nearest grove of old oak trees.] Yet he recognizes that Prudence, indeed, will dictate that Governments long established should not be changed for light and transient Causes; and accordingly all Experience hath shewn, that Mankind are more disposed to suffer, while Evils are sufferable, than to right themselves by abolishing the Forms to which they are accustomed. [A simple survey of these United States over the last decade or two should serve as a clear and humble example of that.] But when a long Train of Abuses and Usurpations evinces a Design to reduce them under absolute Despotism, it is their Right, it is their Duty, to throw off such Government, and to provide new Guards for their future Security. Such has been the patient Sufferance of these Colonies, the subsequent states, and their Conurbations; and such is now the Necessity which constrains them to alter their former Systems of Government. The History of the present Situation is a History of repeated Injuries and Usurpations, all having in direct Object the Establishment of an absolute Tyranny over these

States. To prove this, let Facts be submitted to a candid World.

THEY have refused their Assent to Laws, the most wholesome and necessary for the public Good.

Yet THEY have also conspired to create Bogus Laws that have nothing whatsoever to do with the public Good. One senator from Georgia, in particular, fighting for legislation that would require the posting of the Ten Commandments in public buildings and courthouses, could not—when confronted in a television interview—*name them*.

THEY have called together their Legislative Bodies in Causes unusual, uncomfortable, and distant from the Multitude of the public's true Concerns, for the sole Purpose of fatiguing them into Compliance with their Measures.

THEY have endeavoured to prevent the Population of these States by Certain races; for that Purpose obstructing the Laws for Naturalization of Foreigners; and refusing to pass others to encourage their Migrations hither, making it more difficult and more expensive for decent citizens to have their roofs reshingled, lawns mowed, dishes washed, and, particularly, for members of their own Political Persuasion to have their children cared for cheaply.

THEY have made Judges dependent on their Will alone, for the Tenure of their Offices, and the Amount and Payment of their Salaries.

THEY have erected a Multitude of new Offices, and sent hither Swarms of Officers to harrass our People [especially in the Department of Motor Vehicles], drown them in impenetrable paper work [especially when it comes to the Internal Revenue Service], and generally to eat out our Substance and Sanity.

THEY have plundered our Seas, ravaged our Coasts, burnt our Towns, and destroyed the Lives of our People, [figuratively speaking... except when literally so].

THEY are, at this Time, paying under the Table small Armies of Mercenaries to compleat the Works of Death, Desolation, and Tyranny, already begun with circumstances of Cruelty and Perfidy, scarcely paralleled in the most barbarous Ages, and totally unworthy of the Heads of a civilized Nation.

THEY have excited domestic Insurrections amongst friends and even family members who argue constantly over which Political Party holds the blame for the meltdown of their 401Ks and pension plans, the loss of their jobs, and the death of God... and have endeavoured to bring on the Inhabitants of our Frontiers, the merciless Drug Cartel Savages, whose known Rule of Warfare, is an undistinguished Destruction, of all Ages, Sexes and Conditions.

IN every stage of these Oppressions I have Petitioned for Redress in the most humble Terms [which would of course be, Poetry]: My repeated Petitions have been answered only by repeated Injury and a good deal of Rancorous Nonsense. A Government—whose Character is thus marked by every act which may define a Tyrant, crossed with a 5th Grade Bully—is unfit to be the Grand Poobah of a free People.

NOR have I been wanting in Attentions to my Two-Faced Brethren. [One face for the election, another for the Hill]. I have warned them from Time to Time, in my poetry, of Attempts by their Legislature to extend an unwarrantable "appearance" of Education, Credibility, and Concern for the public Good over us. I have tried to remind them, in my books and essays, of the Circumstances of our Emigration and Settlement here. But, alas, I worry that, one, I might have been too figurative and, two, they may not really be into reading all that much. [Reference the Ten Commandments example above.] I have appealed to their native Justice and Magnanimity, and I have conjured them by the Ties of our common Kindred to disavow these Usurpations, but I'm afraid the word Magnanimity is too big for them and that [since I live all the way out here in Oklahoma] they simply cannot see or hear me. They too have been deaf to the Voice of Justice and of Consanguinity. But, again, we have the big word problem. I must, therefore, acquiesce in the Necessity, which denounces my Separation, and hold them, as I hold the rest of Mankind, Enemies in War, in Peace, Friends.

I, therefore, the Representative of the **united Minions of My Mind,** in General Congress with myself, Assembled, appealing to the Supreme Judge of the World for the Rectitude of my Intentions, do, in the Name, and by Authority of the better Minds throughout History who have explained all of this again and again in the Great Texts, solemnly Publish and Declare, That these United Minions are, and of

Right ought to be, **Vexed and Despondent** over the power-crazed Greed of the politicians in these great States and their absolute impotence when it comes to working through legislation that would benefit the People more than it would their chances of getting re-elected; that I am absolved from all Allegiance to their Lying and Double-Dealing ways, and that all political Connection between them and all that I Hope for the Future of my Daughter's Country and World, is and ought to be totally dissolved; and that as a Vexed and Despondent Citizen, I have full Power to levy Disgust over their Campaign Tactics, conclude Embarrassment over their Ridiculous Partisan Childishness, contract Alliances with Friends and Others who still have living, breathing Consciences to speak of, and to do all other Acts and Things which Despondent Citizens may of right do.—And for the support of this Declaration, with a firm Reliance on the Protection of divine Providence, profane Passion, and General Concern for the Human Race, as well as all other Species, I, the Minions of My Mind, my Friends, and Others of Conscience, mutually pledge to each other our Lives, our Fortunes, our Legacy to our Children, and our sacred Honor.

Nathan Brown.

Know What I Mean?

Button, Elbridge, and Step
are a few of the first names
of our Founding Fathers...
those signers of the Declaration
we love to venerate so much.

I'm sure they were gentlemen.
But with first names like those,
one has to wonder about their
"early histories"—something,
in other words, of their juvenile
and/or delinquent pasts.

Take my dad's hometown,
Cyril, Oklahoma, for instance,
and some of the folks he grew up with:
Skeeter and Dinky... Toots and Wash.

Tell me they weren't up to somethin'
when they were skinny teenagers.

Look... I'm just sayin'...

I'd be curious to hear just what
some of their Founding Mothers
would have to say about
our Founding Fathers.

Making Amends

...according to their respective Numbers, which shall be determined by adding to the whole Number of free Persons, including those bound to Service for a Term of Years, and excluding Indians not taxed, three fifths of all other Persons.

—*The Constitution of the United States of America, Article. I. Section. 2.*

I'm surprised
the Founding Fathers
couldn't see them coming...
all those Amendments to the Constitution...

that those Persons they considered fractions
wouldn't want, someday, down the road,
to be counted as Whole...

or that the Excluded might want to keep
the land we were prying them from...

and that Women—so uncounted
as to even escape mention—
might not desire the Privilege
to vote their Founding Asses
straight out of office.

LIKE THE BIBLE

*They shall in all Cases, except Treason, Felony and Breach of the
Peace, be privileged from Arrest during their Attendance at the
Session of their respective Houses, and in going to and returning
from the same;*

> —*The Constitution of the United States
> of America, Article. I. Section. 6.*

The good Fathers
made other mistakes.
But this one was big

and eventually gave rise
to the most sweetly ensconced
criminal class in these United States,
save... maybe... the Italian mafia.

But what can we do about it?
It's in the Constitution...
that favorite Flag of good citizens
and wannabe patriots to wave
in the faces of whichever party
they hate most at the moment...

this belovéd rolled up newspaper,
wielded by wealthy rock stars
and deer processors alike...

a paper that many
have never read.

BEING USEFUL

To promote the Progress of Science and useful Arts, by securing for limited Times to Authors and Inventors the exclusive Right to their respective Writings and Discoveries;

—*The Constitution of the United States of America, Article. I. Section. 8.*

So, what committee determines
which Arts are useful?

And what would be the required
qualifications for such a group?

By the way, am I alone in thinking
that science should be useful too?

Is the reason government no longer
supports the "Progress of Art"
because so much of it is "useless?"

Let's not mention names. Though,
Thomas Kinkade comes to mind.
And language poetry. Anyway...

this is the strongest urge
I have felt to date
to serve my country
in some capacity.

Ashes over the Southwest

2005

Out here in the middle,
where the center's on the right.

~ James McMurtry

GRANDMA

"Boy!" she hollered,
"come on in out from unner that car!
    It's time f'r lunch!"

I cocked my head and counted:

on – in – out – from – under

Awed by her ability with language,
and still full from breakfast, I thought,

Now, who else could do that...
    just rattle out five prepositions in a row
    without even thinking about it?

And somehow I knew what she meant.

I watched oil creep down my hand
and pondered my degree in linguistics.
All those textbooks and phonetic symbols.
And Grandma? A total mystery.

Like when I was eight years old
and she took me out to the garden
through a banging screen door
to show me our supper,

    "all growed up
        outta God's ground."

Almost

What I had so feverishly longed for then she had been ready, if only I had been able to understand and to meet her again, to let me taste in my boyhood.

—Marcel Proust, *Time Regained*

Didn't think I'd find it,
coming back on Highway 9.
I wanted to swing by your old house
near the lake, my old ginger bread hut
hidden in the forbidden forest.

I remembered 60th over to Lindsey.
Then, I saw the green street sign—
Flaming Oaks—draped in limbs,
and it all came back in a dry flash,
body humming, fingers trembling.
From there, the car drove straight to it,
tires crunching thirsty dirt clods.

I felt again the roaring waves
of that old-time Baptist guilt...
and the heat from hormonal fires
we tried to put out with gasoline.

I remember climbing through the window
in the thrill and terror of a teenage dream,
coming around the edge of your bed,
staring down in unspeakable gratitude
at the threadbare sheet that almost
covered your breasts, knowing

that was all there was
between us.

Your exposed arm and leg…
the moon painting them in milk…
threw my mind into desperate imaginings
of what lay beneath the folds, the lost
and found lines of draping cotton.

I smiled at the cliché of a sleeping princess.
Or maybe you weren't asleep.
Maybe you pretended,
admiring my admiration.

When I finally succumbed,
leaning down to kiss your neck,
your arms wrapped… eyes still closed…
around my twinging shoulders
in a soft swarm of biology,
dreamily pulling me in
to the pool of your expectant form.

We darted in and out
of dangerous corridors,
danced on mossy graves,
denied that final bliss
for fear of blindness
and divine disappointment.

> To get it back. Just one night.
> The ropes that would unravel.

A NOTE OF THANKS

I am terribly grateful to this morning's
low plains snow storm, a Vesuvian
display that floats in so softly, silently,
to dust the flatlands with rapturous inactivity.

What command, with a single powdery hand,
to be able to halt all the silly motions
and illusory dreams of commerce.

My kitchen table, a window onto whiteness,
a cup of tea, a bowl of oats, and crunchy toast—
the stuff of an earthly heaven—are a river
of love and letters onto these white pages.

THINKING ABOUT DEATH

Lately, I've wondered whether
or not I want some gravesite
for young poets to come visit,
leaving prayers and promises
in the cracks of my tombstone
while solemnly contemplating
the business of worms.

Grand delusions aside, cremation
seems more my style, scattered
in fourths among the Arbuckles,
Southern Rockies, Sangre de Cristos,
and Big Bend, the four chambers
of my road-worn, vagabond heart.

As in life, so in death…
I want 'em to have a hard time
finding me.

PEELING ORANGE

At six, visiting my parents,
she plays with silky scarves
and Gammar's woolen hats
in the floor of their fixed-up
and furnished attic.

Orange construction paper flies
from slicing blades to be glued and
slapped onto a larger piece of white.

She staples together unwritten books
from some old business stationary,
showing me the sad magnitude
of its previous uselessness.

Leotards and lacy skirts bounce
and dance in the wake of symphonies,
a blaze of crinkled whiteness
wiping clean centuries of dull
academic talk about Beethoven.

But soon new school friends
will bring on the parental push-off—
        friends possibly denied the bright red
        toolbox of childhood's imagination—

and the orange construction paper
will fade even further to brown,
as it's been doing since my childhood.

And Beethoven will morph into
an exposé of belly buttons writhing
on VH-1's "All Belly Buttons,
All the Time" channel.

So, dad writes a poem
destined for his attic in hope
that someday, long from now,
from a certain loss or sadness,
she'll be driven up there
for the sake of sifting, alone,
and crack open this orange journal…
that I could have left blank…
and find these words.

Maybe her tears will fall
into mine, and she'll remember
the orange construction paper
I'm caressing at the moment,
because
                    I've come home.

I WAS THERE
Friday – July 4, 2003

in red gym shorts and a white T-shirt
pulled up over blue pajama pants.

My little girl, on her bike
that we'd smothered in white
crepe-paper, red bows, and flags,
revved an imaginary engine,
her front tire almost touching
the bumper of the police car
that would lead the parade.

4th of July is a simple holiday
for Oklahoma Sooner fans.
Just add blue to whatever
clothes and cars you already have.

I was there for my daughter
who at seven was thoroughly
drunk on the thrill of being
"in" a parade, rather than
watching from the curb.

I was there for my friend, a soldier
serving us well, even though his eyes
are dots at the bottom of two big
question marks—sober punctuation
on his thoughts about our government.

I was there for my country,
dancing cautiously along in the fever
of maniacal arrogance that builds

to a degree more than hot enough
to burn down Rome a second time.

I was there for Independence,
liberty, and justice for all concerned
that President Bush and his Vice
just might be the most
dangerous men
in the world.

THE TWIG

The name "Jay" is what I remember—
a witty, hands-in-pockets hallway shuffler
at Norman High our senior year in '83.

We carved out survival in the inevitable clan
of skinny misfits that the puberty gods create
in all high schools to balance out jocks and poms.

Nobody could ever come back on Jay.
Their stunted intellects were no match
for his detached scrape of jeans on floor.

He was so casual about it though,
inside his sideways, self-effacing laugh
that always turned his eyes out windows.

Somewhere in the post cap-and-gown days
some unstoppable shadow overtook him.
A twig snapped in the back of his skull.

The dislodged lobes floated apart,
the psychiatrist said. At least that's what
another ex-misfit reported years later.

And Jay's just entered the café where I write,
twenty years out from our adjacent lockers.
He walks slowly... so cautiously now...

looking for the driftwood of his mind
with his one unglazed eye, nodding
up and down, rolling from side to side.

He sits down a few tables over, pushes
bits of iced cinnamon roll through
a bush of red beard and moustache,

all 300 pounds wrapped up
in a swaddling of thrift coats...
his eyes... still out the window...

and I'm missing something too.

PRICE OF ADMISSION

Something about a Saturday night football game—
suspended for fifty minutes at the end of the first
quarter because of pouring rain and lightning.
Something about the goose bumps and raindrops on
the beautifully tanned shoulders and arms of girls
caught by the weather—the smell of it all dripping to
dirty concrete along with the ketchup and mustard
overloaded onto foot-and-a-half-long corndogs.
Something about that sudden mid-September drop
in temperature that makes you want to wrap your
arms around those shivering shoulders—no
commitment intended—just to... you know... take
one for the team. Something about that third quarter
interception and runback by the new freshman
whose adrenalin speed clips the heels of the storm's
lightning and the fan's rolling thunder that follows.
Something about a plastic tray of nachos sacrificed
on the pavement by a thousand shoe soles, then
baptized in Coke, leaving only faint traces of sliced
jalapeños. I don't know what brings me here. But the
corndog alone is worth the price of the ticket I paid
too much for, there on the sidewalk, five minutes
before kickoff.

S/U – ATHLETE EVALUATIONS

I am to teach them English.
And I am to evaluate
performance at mid-semester.

Of the three: one listens,
laughs at my jokes, but rides
the razor's edge at "C-"—
a good kid, disarmingly polite;

another is a blow-off,
no notebook in class,
didn't get a course packet,
leaves like a prince
out of parliament
to go to the bathroom,
and did fairly well
on the essay exam;

the third sleeps sitting up,
eyes open, never completed
a sentence in his essay,
can't possibly pass without
that great, smiling social worker
of college athletes: plagiarism.

And the form reads:
satisfactory=S
unsatisfactory=U
But the law in Oklahoma is:
Love the college football player
aS yoU love yoUrself.

Visitors' Guide

Calvin is my town's "paper boy."
He wears a crimson batter's helmet
with a grid-like football mask attached—
a big white 36 stenciled on the back.

He's on a first name basis
with 100,000 people it seems,
as he beats the main drags
with his over-the-shoulder
"Norman Transcript" bag.
The price is a quarter.
Everyone gives a buck.

He used to be shy in his slowness.
But several years ago, some local-boy-
gone-big made a movie called *Possums*
and based a character on Calvin.

Ever since, he's owned the place.
His twisting monotone has increased
in volume, and he graciously pities
those less fortunate than he, cracking
jokes with businessmen and politicians.

If you ever decide to visit, take care
where one thing is concerned:
never touch the helmet.

I watched some frat pledge from Texas
reach out in faux admiration once.
Three big locals grabbed the idiot
and jerked him away, while Calvin—

arms raised in jaguar defense—
backed out of the café
and down the sidewalk on Main.

The locals told the kid:
Do it again…
> *and we'll kick your ass.*

HE LIVES ROUND HERE

I barely know him—but,
enough to sense the pressure
behind his punctured voice,
barely able to complete a sentence
for fear of its inevitable
lack of coherency.

Something happened back there.
A throat-slit of well-aimed words
cast his eyes to the floor
where they mostly remain,
only occasionally making
efforts to rise and meet you,
as if a memory made of brick
were tied to a hole in each eyelid.

Dressed all in baggy black,
with bleached hair, he bounces
behind a musical wall—
head bowed behind
a stack of keyboards,
some salvation train
he believes he's on.

Certain notes, a touch too loud,
are his spasmodic screams back
at the faces of what happened.

Someday, through the scales,
he may even find the key
to the rusted iron door of grace.

Being alive is his ticker-tape parade,
his testament to survival, his hope
for the resurrection of buried eyes.

LASTING IMPRESSIONS

I. Waitress in Boston:

"So, where's the accent from?"
Oklahoma. Where's yours from?
"What? Well... you're just... a lot nicer
than I thought Oklahomans would be."

◆　◆　◆

II. Yosi, in Jerusalem:

"Are you still having problems
with the Indians there?"

◆　◆　◆

III. Vitale – Russian Olympic Rugby Player and
Local Guide in Chimkent, Kazakhstan:

"Amerikanski Cowboyskis!"

◆　◆　◆

IV. Three Israeli Soldiers at the Southern
Checkpoint into the West Bank:

1 - "Let dem go."
2 - "No no! Dis bad."
3 - "No matter."
1 - "Where from?"
Oklahoma.
1 - "?"

Texas?
2 - "Ma?"
  Dallas?
3 - "Oh! Dallas! J Rrrr Ewing! You know?"
  Yeah… uh… he's my uncle.
1 - "Let dem go."

◆　　◆　　◆

V. Waiter at Sam's in San Francisco:

"And, where are you from?"
  Oklahoma.
"Ohmygod."

ONE HOUR

Here where the chrome pin
fits tightly into the very last notch
of the Bible Belt wrapped wide
around the fat belly
of a nation stuffed with
Christians and cock-fighters,

there's hardly a car or pickup
on the streets from 11am to noon
on Sundays—a fabulous time
to go for a walk, catch God
on his cigarette break.

BURN

Oklahoma in July
is a marshmallow
in a bonfire...

a branding iron
on the face...

a toad in the slow-
ly heated pot,

where Fahrenheit
screams until its eyes
turn red—

until the blood
rises in its mercurial veins.

A Defining Dilemma

Just bought the *Oxford English Dictionary*
on CD-ROM; Second Edition; Version 3.0.
It cost me 319 dollars and 71 cents.

I look at the box on my table and think:
    900 years of changes in words and language,
    50 years of collecting them into this work...
    and the majority of the definitions
    came from a doctor-gone-mad-serial-killer
    that the editors never met, but trusted
    was a scholar slaving away in a garret,
    as opposed to some asylum.

But, what's the shock... really...
considering the psychological history
of excessive scholarly research?

LOWLAND HERETIC

Down by the base of a wheat stalk
in the well-tended fields of the Lower
Great Plains' Republicans, I lie…

a brown slithering Democrat,
narrowly escaping the occasional blaze
of buckshot and boot soles at cockfights—
roosters with razor blades.

Once buried in the holy waters
of a good Southern Baptism
at the age of seven,

I now raise
a sinful hand up and out toward
the softly shaking head of St. Jude

in hopes he'll rescue this lonely lost cause
from the rage of a red-faced denomination
that lords an iron domination
over the souls of good people

who can't see the fat
clogging its veins
and arteries.

KNOWING BETTER

She sneaks in around 7 a.m.,
slips into the other side of the bed—
angel of seven sweet years—
and we sleep until 8:30.

Her sleep, sound. Mine,
the nervous sleep of a dad
remembering the thoughts
of little eight, nine, and ten-
year-old boys—punks. They are.
We were. I was…. hormones like
unpopped corn slowly heating in oil.

◆　　◆　　◆

I give up, shuffle into the kitchen
to pour apple juice and consider
having her discreetly followed
by a bodyguard for eleven years.

She follows, a few minutes later,
yawning, rubbing eyes, still trusting
the world, believing life might be
the rainbows and pots of gold
promised in her colorful books.

◆　　◆　　◆

Over cereal she prays aloud
that God will know we love him
and appreciate the toast with grape jelly.

I pray, lips pressed together, that God
will part the inevitabilities of time
like the Red Sea and drown all
the teenaged boys in our wake,

knowing her prayer is truer than mine,
and that Jesus is smiling at her
with one disapproving eye shot my way.

INTER-DIMENSIONAL THRIFT-SHOPPING

At the next table… two sisters,
both with long gray hair swirled up
and bobby pinned in untidy buns.

Two guys, one painting a glop
of white ceramic art; the other
eating macaroni pie left-handed.

The first sister talks about dreams
mingling with reality, and butcher
knives mingling with her ex's chest.

The painter follows with a few tips
from Buddha… and Freud… and
some possible mild medications,

never looking up from his fine-
tipped brush… his armpits
darkening from August sweat.

The second sister speaks of Jesus
and the time the first sister tried
to kill her in their parents' house.

They had both been so religious.
And the first sister waves it off
and tells the painter she'd gotten

something at the Wiccan place
to calm her down. And she thinks
she's doing a bit better now.

The lefty then interjects that
he'd spent 20 years stoned, and...
now his boy lives in Colorado...

and his little girl's down in Florida
somewhere. And the second sister
immediately steps in with the fact

that the daughter she had not seen
for five years "appeared" next to her
in the Goodwill store this morning,

and the lady behind the counter
saw her too and asked a question
about her. And a long discussion

ensues with the four around the table
about whether or not this was a good
thing. And the eventual consensus

seems to be that it was, and that
this was her daughter's way of
bringing their spirits together.

And the sister is so glad,
because she'd bought a couple
of Indian dolls for the apparition—

you know... as a gift, little altars,
in honor of their afternoon of
inter-dimensional thrift-shopping.

CRITICAL CARE

I caught her out the corner of my eye
and quickly pushed the OPEN DOOR
button to let her in, a grandma trying
to hide the twitch of worry in her cheeks.

Both on our way to the second floor...
the Critical Care Unit. I jingled keys.
She gripped two huge McDonalds sacks
in one wrinkled, white-knuckled hand.

I, almost forgetting where I was,
almost said, *C'mon Mam, you know
that stuff is why most of us are here;
why it's harder for them to find a vein.*

But she's from a time and a place
that demand, when someone is sick,
and families are paralyzed with fear,
you go and get them food and drink.

And she's right. And while we feed
the hurting their comfort, McDonalds
feeds doctors their business, and all
have a place in the great circle of life.

THE WORK OF HEAVEN

Sooner Football kicks off
tomorrow, doubling the size
of our little town—locals
and shop-owners bustling
around like coastal villagers
preparing for a hurricane.

Crimson & Cream flags
hang out windows, line streets,
car dealerships… and they flap
just above the doors of every
Dodge Ram Dooley and
battered Datsun in sight.

And Jubal sounds reveille
as God rolls out of bed,
cracks his knuckles,
and prepares to detail ranks
of jittery angels about the coming
conflict in the prayers of players…

their mothers and grandmothers,
who will be praying against
the mothers and grandmothers
of players on the opposing team,
and how someone must lose,
and how heaven must choose,
and that it's a dirty business,
but, *It is what we get paid for.*

HONESTLY,

I'm 38-and-a-half years old,
and she still packs little ice chests
and picnic baskets for my road trips,
right down to the red and white
checkered napkins and plastic-ware.

And I want to tell her,
I have money now, mom...
I've learned to shop, don't eat
at McDonalds anymore. But,
I don't because I love her food.

Here at the tail end of a PhD,
she still follows me to the door
of the house I grew up in, forcing
Ziploc Baggies of frozen bread
into my already stuffed hands
while telling me how to know when
things have gone bad in the fridge.
Her face betrays a genuine fear
that I'll eat the expired and die.

And I want to tell her, I've had
20 years of higher ed now, mom,
and I've finally figured out
the whole mold thing, the smell
of bad meat... and bad people.
But, I don't because I need the bread,
and I'm pretty sure I ate something
a little funky a few days ago.

I've already lived longer than Christ did,
and I've still gotta eat my veggies
when I have dinner with her and dad.

And I want to tell her, longevity is not
one of the hallmarks of my profession.
But, I don't because I know I need
the fiber... and, besides, nothing
in the universe can stand up to the sheer
force and power of a mother's love.

AFTER

I walk in the sigh of evening, the deep breath
that follows the flash of a summer thunder storm.
The sodium orange of sidewalk lights
almost matches the fringe of the cloud line.

Faces appear, as if from a flooded anthill.
Smiles break out in the strangeness of the cool.
Friends, unknown until this vernal moment
greet each other in a sudden camaraderie.

Fins and fishing poles salute each other
in respect to the cycles of life.
Squawking ducks and squealing children
with bread dance in a circle of giving.

A damp breeze coaxes the smell of beans
and cornbread from an open window.
It mingles with the oily pavement
and the must of rain-drenched wood.

Even in the dying light, though,
distant flashes remind me—
clouds will come to storm again
but only to revive the pulse of life.

QUIET REUNION

Santa Fe is a favorite escape. But,
I hear an increase in its groans and sighs…
a much heavier stress on its spine
from the profit and decay that always
seep into the most beautiful spaces
when discovered by wealthy tourists.

And though I've arrived at the peak
of pork season, with its gaudy Hawaiian shirts
and white calves above black socks and sandals,
it's also the tail-end of a bleak, blistering year
in which my soul has been holding up
my frail body and its embattled spirit.

Still, I'm happy to see my old friend.
It's just a quieter reunion than usual.
More like I've asked her not to make
any special plans this time around—
no fanfare or fancy spreads—
just time to rest our tired souls
against each other.

I'll bitch & moan about my terrorists.
She'll bitch & moan about her tourists.
And then we'll raise a toast at sunset
on the top floor patio of La Fonda—

To hell with 'em all…

SMACKING THE CORE

The rotting apple core that is my life
these days followed me to Santa Fe.

It hovers around my stomach
like an obstinate bee as I sit
in a favorite coffee shop to write,
struggling to endure what has been,
in the past, an easy joy.

It plops along behind me
in the thin back alleys, splashing
in putrid, iridescent pools, laughing
at my childish insecurity, smelling
a bit worse with each grungy bath.

It even followed me into Longevity Café...
paradise on earth... and tried to spoil
my Vietnamese Spring Rolls.

But then, I ordered, in defiance,
the Ginseng Chai Pumpkin Pie
with Soy Dream Ice Cream.

It was as if I had smacked the core
in the middle of its jiggling seeds...
sent it sprawling into the far corner
of the orange and red room.

I ate with avarice, glaring.
And the core huddled in the corner,
shaking, afraid maybe I would
stride over and smack it again.

AN OKIE MINGLES

La Plazuela
en La Fonda.

My usual table
in the back corner,
just out of the sunlight.

Enchiladas del Norte
y sangría con una
fresh yellow palm daisy
next to my vaso de agua.

The rough stone floor
slopes toward la mesa
in front of me where
a gray haired madre
y una hija linda
share lonche en paz
and conversation.

La hija is a
magazine cover.
But la madre es
mas bonita a me.

Something she knows,
something vieja.

Something that holds
her shoulders back,
and her daughter
en su corazón.

A Palpable Patron

It's tough to maintain
a patron saint
when you've grown up
a Baptist preacher's kid.

But, when you've got one,
you've got one...
Catholic or not.

St. Jude, patron saint
of lost causes—intercessor
of desperate situations—
made himself known to me
over the last couple of years...

came to me knowing I would
not, being a Baptist, come
to him. And I appreciate it.

Turns out, I needed him.

Why should it surprise me, though,
    God
reaching over denominational walls.

PROTOCOL

I'm not exactly sure
how this saint thing works
on a technical level.

I just know
that when my
theological questions
grow feathers and
collect like cottonseed
in the air conditioner,

> and it feels like God has left
> for Latvia because he needs
> a break from Southern Baptists,

it's nice to have someone
to talk to.

HOLY JOKES

An old man in Taos once told me
that countries and cities have
patron saints too. Peru has Joseph.
Paris, Genevieve. But when he got to

these United States, he said:
    Immaculate Conception.
I cocked my head in a question mark,
smiling with only the left corner

of my mouth. I could have sworn
I heard a distant, taunting laughter
echoing all the way from the halls
of Rome—a kick from Italy's boot.

Yes. America, America: a land
gorged on the belief of its own
holy birth... blessed above other
nations... defied on penalty of death.

No room for a humble, humiliated
Christ here among corporate mergers,
ordained politicians, and reincarnated
crusaders against the forces of evil.

Renovations at the
Santuario de Guadalupe

Jesus is on his back
on the grand piano while
workers repaint the santuario.

He's an old, time-worn
piece of wood with chips
on the knees, one on the forehead—
white scabs on one tough man-God.

The painters reach to turn off
the wail of mariachi music
on a white-splattered radio,
so we can discuss sacred images.

And I notice, through the scaffolding,
the nails look as if they go through
his feet, the cross, and into the piano,

and his head, normally bowed
when the cross is upright,
looks now as if
he's trying to get up.

SANTUARIO DE CHIMAYÓ

The tears of last year's prayers,
prayed in this very spot,
well up in my sore eyes—
lids and lashes like sandbags
that can't hold the rising river.

Soaked villagers stand on muddy hills
in my mind and watch the homes
and stores fill with brown water as
cars and bicycles twist and wash away.

The prayers for protection and healing were
answered, but now sit like moving boxes
piled in the corners of my heart, abandoned
because of indecision. So, one by one,
while resting in this rough-hewn pew,
I open boxes and watch my trust in God
scatter like a panic of doves.

Jesus weeps
and smiles at the same time
in the face of every crucifix
in the sanctuary.

And I smear the dirt of a miracle
on my forehead and wrists
while Christ wipes my tears
with a bloody thumb, then opens
his other hand towards the door.

I walk out into a different shade of light,
weak from a baptism few Baptists
could ever understand while gathered
in the shadows of their giant crosses
in the giant parking lots of their giant
churches out in the suburbs of heaven.

Jemez Springs

Think Rain! screams a green sign
nailed to a bent tree across the road.

    I glance back and forth from the sign
    to the angry clouds boiling up over
    the mountains in every direction.

After the last bite of spinach n' mushroom burrito
on the screened-in porch of the Laughing Lizard,
I'm surprised I'm still dry, the sky having grumbled
like a bad stomach through my entire meal.

But not even the Jemez thunder can squeeze
a drop to slake the devastating drought…

    just like the Paraclete down the road
    couldn't help the problem priests that
    everyone thought were here to dry out
    from an addiction to sacramental wine,
    but, as it turned out, were here because
    of their penchant for little altar boys…

    just like Father Mac—the one guy
    some locals think might have been
    trying to heal the horrid situation—
    couldn't stop the doped-up maniac
    from bludgeoning him to death,
    even though he put up a fight…

    a maniac who went on to claim
    he'd been abused…   a claim

no one at the time thought to check
against his attendance record.

And my eyes come back to the sign
nailed to the tree, and I think about Jesus

and about all the priests later released
into the shadows of the red rock mesas
and surrounding hills full of little boys...

right about the time my waiter
steps back over and smudges
all the fresh ink of my thoughts
with *his* summary of it all:

Some creepy shit, man.

Remember Los Alamos

Best part's the drive in.
The town itself leaves me
a little dry, like every time
my president utters "nuc-u-lar"
for the type of weapons
everyone else should not have.

I'm sure there's something
at its core, something cool
like winter, or a hot nightlife,
but I can't find it.

I turn right on Oppenheimer Road
hoping something will explode
into view, but it only goes 100 feet,
then dead ends at the public library.

While sippin' heavy coffee in Café Allegro,
a huge Peach Granola Muffin just glows
with flavor like there was a great big buttery
meltdown in the back of the kitchen.

A Japanese family sits two tables over—
two fabulous daughters with fabulous tattoos.

And the bumper sticker on the register reads:

LOS ALAMOS
BIRTHPLACE OF THE BOMB

But We Want To

We never quite touch,
outside of those occasional
light slaps with the backs of our fingers
on the other's shoulder, eyes going wide
in a smile, as if to say *I can't believe
you just said that!* when, really
you do,
you do believe it,
and you want to believe
in that and much more,
even love.

We never quite kiss,
in the moment when we pause
beneath the acacia tree in the plaza,
Christmas lights dangling from branches,
subdued in the distant glow
of St. Francis Cathedral.

Not even when our eyes meet,
lock, and linger in desperation,
because we know the ropes
and chains back home will lead
to separate cages, like the endings
of every Shakespeare play combined.

We never quite say it,
because words fall like leaves
to the ground and drift away
in the late summer rains
of this ancient town.

SHITS IN THE SHED

"Poets are shits,"
Tony Mares told me
over Golden Margaritas
at The Shed... told me
that's what his third wife
told him over—quite possibly—
margaritas when they first met...

this one being the marriage
that has worked the best
for him so far.

And I thought, *Well... yeah...
I mean... I can't fight her on it.*

But isn't this what pairing up
eventually comes down to?

You gotta pick your shit.
Choose one and go with it.

And I must say,
Tony and I were
two   fine   shits
in The Shed that night.

OVER IN THE PLAZA

I sit on a park bench,
knees tucked into my arms.

The breeze is cool in the wake
of an evening thunderstorm.

The clock on the corner of Palace
and Lincoln softly glows 10:30—

same time as the night we passed
through the square like two moons

in and out of patchy clouds, much like
the sky's moon does right now.

Loud-talkers laugh and screech
over beers on The Ore House balcony.

Two policemen stand, hands in pockets,
on the corner of Lincoln and San Francisco,

and two city workers clear off chairs
in front of the stage across from

the Palace of the Governors, as if
something is over and not coming back.

That's when I see a couple kiss beneath
the lights strung in the acacia tree.

And that's when I have to leave, because
something is over, and it's not coming back.

ROAD TO NINEVEH

As I blow down
the inside lane of I-35
and cross the Red River—

tainted by Moses' divine dipstick—
I see a mighty storm a blowin',
racing up behind me.

So I quickly move over
to let it pass—looks like
maybe a preacher's wife,

in a nutshell brown Caddy,
late for a Friday evenin' potluck
designed to keep men out of bars.

There's just enough time to read
the license plate—"PRAISEM"

I toy with the grammar a bit...
until I get lost somewhere in Denton
and have to make a U-turn at Scripture Street.

PERDITION

I sat on a beautiful lawn chair
on the beautiful back porch
overlooking the beautiful pool
of the beautiful home
of my beautiful friends
in Dallas.

And, all the while,
the incessant growling,
hacking and coughing,
of an industrial-sized
Asplundh tree-mulcher roared

and sprayed its wooden sputum
into the back of a diesel-humming
orange and black truck,
like some sick, anachronistic,
metal mastodon—

as if the twenty first century
needed to add a new circle
to Dante's raging hell
in order to keep up with
the magnitude and volume
of its planet-sodomizing sins.

My friends are moving to the Hill Country.

SAN MARCOS

The grit and hipness in this town
stares you down like the glowing tips
of cigarettes between every first
and second finger of every hand
in The Coffee Pot, where I sit

by the window looking out across
the street at Lady Justice holding
the scales atop the courthouse,
suffocating in a thick glaze of silver
like a cheap version of the girl in *Goldfinger*,

or like the cloud around the girl next to me
with her head tilted towards textbooks,
but like, talkin' on her cell phone, like
she's not too young to be, like, smoking
and, like, drinking coffee, you know?

And I wonder if her dad's a cowboy
like the bronze statue of a horseman
there on the corner of LBJ & Hopkins
who through the haze in this place appears
to have smoke pourin' from the barrel
of his pistol pointed up at the big Texas sky

as if to say *Don't come down here... don't
even pass through these here parts...
unless yer serious...
ya' damn Okie.*

HIGHWAY 24

I cut through the heart
of Colorado today.

Highway 24...
cheesecake of America:
thick sliceable frosting
    of layered snow...
atop a black forest filling
    of spruce and pine...
with a rich brown needle crust...

nature's way of fighting to keep
the fundamentalist hordes
that have flocked to this state
home from Sunday School.

And I zipped right by
a roadside marquee
that jerked my neck
back for a second:

"Revival Canceled"

SIMILE

/'sImIlI/ *n.* 1. esp. poetical comparison of one thing with
another using the words 'like' or 'as' (e.g. *as brave as a lion*).
2 use of this. [Latin, neuter of *similes* like]
           —The Oxford Dictionary of Current English

I've been trying to think of a simile
      that would do justice to

that slow drive home
after that storybook first date
where your arms occasionally bump—
      because you're wanting to touch
      but are afraid of being overt—
while walking over the bridges
of a gaspingly romantic town…
like Manitou Springs or something…

and the fact that this is not a good time
in your life to be feeling this way
makes your heart pound against
the wall of practicality even harder
because you know…
      you just know…
           you're sunk,

and all I can come up with is—
      it feels a lot like

that slow drive home
after that storybook first date
where your arms occasionally bump—

because you're wanting to touch
but are afraid of being overt—
while walking over the bridges
of a gaspingly romantic town...
like Manitou Springs or something...

and the fact that this is not a good time
in your life to be feeling this way
makes your heart pound against
the wall of practicality even harder
because you know...
you just know...
you're sunk.

UNITED STATES

Except for the thin membrane
of Oklahoma's Panhandle,
Texas and Colorado almost touch.

On a clear day one could almost see
smoke signals from the other,
drifting up and over Black Mesa
where jackrabbits jet among sage.

◆　　◆　　◆

There is something of the in-between
in this windblown space where my favorite states
hold hands in a tenuous agreement—
    not quite trusting each other,
    but trusting "all else" much less.

There is a quiet hill here
that never forgot the Trojan War,
the Fall of Rome, or the Spanish Inquisition,
because it never knew they happened.

There is a small town here,
Boise City, that knows World War II,
because in '43 a home team B-17
mistook the courthouse lights
for a test range down the road.

◆　　◆　　◆

Here, where Texas almost touches Colorado,
the rocks and stunted trees stand between
states...   between generations...
solid among the arms of the Milky Way.

And that's why this place laughed
that day the power-grid shut down
up in New York City. Folks out here
snorted at their panic and shock...

out here, where a moonless night is so dark,
you can't see the ground beneath your feet.

WHERE I GO

A quiet angel sits
on the southern rim
of a lonely overlook,

a hidden guardian
among the blue
rock and cedars.

She offers rest

to the singer
whose song wilts
in the heat
of an earless audience

to the painter
whose brush hardens
in the primary colors
of market demands

to the poet
whose prophecies
bounce off the doors
of a dying church.

Suffer the Little Voices

2005

*We rebel against Grace
settle for piety.*

~ Ken Hada

This Time the Angel

Stunned,
I go for a walk.

For bigger conundrums
the pond is a good friend.

Half way round,
that shadow again…
the Great Blue Heron…
stands silently on the shore.

I wonder when she'll fly this time.
How close will she let me get?

Strangely,   she stays,
watches cautiously,
lets me pass.

And so… I think maybe
I shouldn't fly away either…
as I've done in the past.

In Numbers, Chapter 22—
the angel is an ass…
    a funny thing
        for an angel to be.

But I'm one to talk.
This time the angel
is a Great Blue Heron.

SOUL-SAVERS

I gaze back at the pain and
disdain we felt for "the lost"
in covert planning sessions
we called Bible studies. Then,

I turn my head away with a jerk
from the sight of my old church
in a weak and strained attempt
to push down this past stupidity—

a stupidity constructed through
millenniums of bad dogma,
which was "not busy livin'…
just busy dyin'," as Bob Dylan,

a theologian of a different cut,
tried to tell us in the years
we couldn't look past his
prophetic, soul-felt addictions.

My sighs and shaking head signify
the inevitable departure from that…
from them… not Jesus [still my favorite
hippie socialist]. But I do realize that…

in the nouns and verbs I now choose
to express myself… I've lost them—
the "they" I once was. And I'm struck
by the new fear that now…

it's *me* they're after.

A GROWING CONCERN

I'm a bit jaded. But
I still tear up every time Linus,
haloed in light, tells Charlie Brown
what Christmas is all about
from that empty school stage.

I admit my cynicism. But
I still pull my blanket up
to wipe my eyes when the bell rings
at the end of *It's a Wonderful Life*.
The little girl makes her proclamation.
Jimmy Stewart smiles up at Clarence.

I often agree with Goethe and Chekov
when they sing of the stupid masses.
But lately, I put my hand over my heart,
sing the national anthem at football games.

And I flat out cry when my daughter
wraps her porcelain arms around the left
pant leg of my jeans and looks up
with blazing blue-gray eyes still void
of all the shadows and doubts
that eat away at mine,

and I find myself slapping
at a creeping, irrepressible urge
to hope.

SAVIORS

Seven, maybe eight
years old, she struggles
with the drawstring
of her funky jeans,
chin on her chest
in frustrated concentration.

Fortyish, give or take,
he walks up and around
from behind... in jeans
and a red baseball hat,
kind eyes, soft knowing smile...
and kneels down to help.

She's not embarrassed,
because he knows
just what to say.
She smiles.
Jesus weeps.

He scratches her brown hair
as he stands up.
They walk away,
two Christmas ribbons
silking in the wind,
attached at the center,

and I wonder how many
worlds could be saved
if more fathers
could be so dad-like.

THE TRAGEDY

After the last shattered fragment
of the grayish hull has stopped
bouncing on the winter-hard brown
of a stubble-covered wheat field...

after the last of the flames
have surrendered to the blanket
of drizzle, applied like a salve
by sentient banks of clouds...

after the last plume of purple smoke
has been swept away by a sudden gust,
desperate to soften the glare
of the apocalyptic scene...

there comes that point, down the road,
when you grab your rebuilt leg, lift
a foot from the wheelchair stirrup,
and touch the earth again.

There comes that point, eventually,
when you grab the rough bark
of the blackjack tree and pull
dead weight onto your legs.

And there even comes the point,
when you try to lift the pen,
pop off the lid and force its tip
down the faint, familiar trail
of paper that speaks softly
of your remembrance.

ASHES TO DUST

I sit on the outskirts
of the last few years
watching the artifices
of a previously peaceful
and somewhat directed life
burn to the ground,
mostly smoke and ashes now,
the thunder of flames
reduced to a coughing
afterthought of all the
smoldering indictments
and popping epithets.

My forefinger quivers,
unconsciously scrapes
at an ashen smudge
on my forearm,
stirring up a quiet,
angelic laughter
at my amazing lapse
in understanding
the laws of heaven,
thinking I could make it
look clean again with enough
time and spit.

I soon leave it
in a sad gesture to remembrance,
and instead use the finger
to draw in the hard-baked sand—
a Messianic counting of sheep,
because shepherding may be

the only thing left to me
in the midst of this new,
Pacific-sized desert
descended from a warped
and brooding troposphere.

Not one of the four
geographic directions
offers a resurrected view now.
So, I look back down and think
maybe I'll start with toes,
because toes
are most familiar
with the honesty
and demands
of dust.

FIREWALKING

There's something about
the knee-bending moments—
attacks on the soul—that force
our noses to the gritty floor
and hold us there until
we wake up to that pesky
and incessant trope:
God is the last bastion.

There's something about
these red-eyed occasions—
a desperate pulse bulging
in our necks—that flings
an entire lifetime's baggage
out into Saturn's rings.

And when we survive, stand,
walk the luminous coals,
wade the Stygian void,
we find a power
that throbs with life
and laughs
in the face of death.

Because, now we've seen
the phosphorescent center.

We no longer demand
cloud-written messages.

The next breath, next step
are signs enough.

EITHER WAY
a note on postmodernism

There comes a point
when one chooses between
"something" and "nothing."

If one chooses nothing,
there's really no need
to waste any time
railing against those who
choose something.

No loss.
A lack of anything
requires no maintenance.

But, if there *is* something,
how can any one who
believes in nothing
blame the one who believes
in something
for proclaiming to the one
who believes in nothing
that there just might be
something
to this something-thing?

TEST

I step into the flames.
Let the burn do its work.

My time with Christ
down in the under.

I breathe as best I can,
unafraid of my fear.

Hair singes away.
Skin turns to coal.

Must wait til it's done.
Then, I'll fall forward

and be dead, or
unstoppable.

CLUTCH

There's
something
about the very
bottom. Something
about not knowing if
you'll make it out alive.
There comes a point when
fear and pain   lose power,
 and you begin   to let go,
   realizing   the only thing
    left is to watch for what
     God will do in his timing.
      You release your grasp
       on dogma, and hope
        grace will hold.

WEAK DEFIANCE

When the news grows fangs…

When the doctor stares at the floor
    before he reads the diagnosis…

When the door swings open to the sunglasses
    of an unsmiling highway patrolman…

Before any words are uttered,
our minds fly away like sparrows
when the back door bangs the frame,
and we flutter off to repaint the walls of hell,
to tidy it up for an early arrival.

In these capsized moments,
we run to the basement
of worst-case scenarios.
It's as innate as drinking water.

This time, though, I'll swim
against the great river—
choose the possibility of good.

The current is strong.
But my arms pound
the torrent of waves.
My feet search
for sand and rock.

A WALL FOR WAILING

I need a wall
this strong to lean
my life against.

Jerusalem stone,
yellowing in the scorch
of history, yet
mighty enough to stand
over millennia,
calming
the manic blur of my mind,
relaxing
the clenched fist of my spirit.

I have no proper hat,
no tassels or curls,
no Torah scroll or phylactery,
but I feel the hand
of something big
urging me forward anyway,
a heavenly breath
of acceptance and
permission,
a love
above the law.

COFFEEHOUSE ANGELS

I know now why people stop eating...
    why Mindy rolls up in her sheets for days
    at a time with the lights out, forearms
    pressing thighs into chest, gently rocking.

I know why people stop washing their hair
one day without apparent reason...
    why Glove Man, when he walks the streets,
    wears multiple layers of clothing
    against invisible fingers that extend out
    from the little voices, causing him to swat
    occasionally in the middle of sideways,
    barely breathed soliloquies to tired angels
    who have given up and sat down
    in the dirt behind him.

I've begun to understand the silent language
the sunburned old lady mouths
at The Cup's back corner table...
    an angel I've avoided until now,
    hair like a neglected hound.

I may hold on to what she let go.
But I know now
               why she did.

And the angels helped her do it.

BLOWING OVER

Religion has pulled her face
down and to the side a bit.

Eyes recede under the weight
of a brow that has so long borne
a concern for the lack of salvation
that surrounds her.

She still walks upright. But,
her shoulders lead out first...

the rest of her body just a band
of frightened, obedient children
trying to keep a measured distance.

She's something like the half
of the tree left standing after
the middle strike of the storm...

and you just know
the next big wind...

WHY

I write.
I want to be read…
heard in spite
of a million emails a minute,
and in spite
of a billion bubble jets spewing
half-lived dreams,
half-thought thoughts. And yet

I gasp in the bulge
of all that goes unsaid,
unwritten,
and the hope it undoes. So

I pray just one time,
maybe twice—
I'd take 21 if granted—
to write in the blood
of my fingers clawing
at the concrete of loss…

in the marrow of my bones
broken on a slab of devotion…

in the juices of my body
poured out in a sacrifice
for the sake of one who,
decades… centuries
beyond my death,
peels these pages,

unafraid to lick them
for a taste, a faint trace
of Golgotha's ink. Then,

with an echo of Messianic
thunder still rolling
in the unquenchable distance,
she slams the book shut,
lights candles, pours wine,
folds back her own cover,
and dips a pen in the tears
of her own Gethsemane.

RESURRECTION

The phone rings at 8:59 am.
And before the second ring,
I relive the last three days
and two nights down below:

as my blood dripped onto test slips,
then—transcribed into seven-syllable
words much like nucleic hieroglyphs
on torch-lit walls in my body—
told the myth of my life and death...

as I lit a Wal-Mart Virgencita candle
and spread pebbles given me
by my daughter, like bones
from a witch doctor's bag...

as I, deep in the entrails of night,
scratched the floor in an effort
to decode divine communiqués
in the flick and bounce
of yellow flames...

as I never quite uttered selfish prayers
for redemption and wholeness,
paralyzed by the needs
of eleven million orphans
of AIDS in Africa... and then...

as I awoke this morning
to a heavy snowfall, a bowl
of corn flakes and banana,
the phone beside my hand,

waiting...

the phone rings at 8:59 am.

Sixty seconds later,
I set it back down.

I turn my eyes to bright windows
and see the reprieve
signed in the tears of angels
on a white blanket of grace
softly covering the barrenness
of a long relentless winter.

In That Moment...

In the moment you turn
from the facts and evidence
on paper and take to staring
at the ceiling fan instead...

in the moment you relax fists
and lower arms in the face
of an oncoming punch...

in the moment words
cease to be the means
of rant and prayer...

in the moment victory
loses its appeal—
feels the same as defeat...

in that moment, you are ready
to live the beautiful life
that only comes from being
ready to die a beautiful death.

THE ORDINATION

Lucifer simply
had a job to do.
His flash and fall
were not an accident
or some angelic fit.

His heroic dive
created thought
and the possibility
for love

as much as
any power
or pair of eyes
left gazing
over heaven's edge
at the necessary
blaze
of his trail.

MISPLACED ANGEL

Two uptown ladies, manicured,
pedicured, headicured, both having
oatmeal with double-shot espressos.

One little girl with long brown hair—
an angel separated from the host—
picks at a bagel with pb n' jelly...
her head bowed beneath
the adult conversation.

Lady one slurps... hopes the sons
of a friend straighten up soon
from the beer and pizza of fraternity;
hopes the girl of another friend
gets a good rush at sorority
so she'll find a good boy in fraternity.

Lady two swigs... drags through details
of the sordid difficulties of her life:
the lime green wallpaper
with a horrid floral pattern
that wallpaper-man is redoing;
the barstools still in the back
of the 70s station wagon
of upholstery-woman who
will not return calls.

Both swoon from disapproval,
shake heads at a disintegrating
world that no longer responds
properly to the whims and desires
of obvious superiority.

And the angel's eyes ping pong
with a dread they can't define,
and so, throw a prayer
across the small space between
clouds of Esteé Lauder base,
a prayer, a question, that I worry
is prayed in my direction
because God is choking
on Dillard's dust:

"Will they return for me?"

ENTROPY

I'm not sure a life begins
until disgrace
enters through some
unlocked door,
runs its leaky course
like an exploding dye
in the spinal column.

Maybe this is why Genesis
begins with a fall...
and goes down from there.

Maybe this is David's insatiable
thirst for failure... Solomon's
kaleidoscopic lament, his passage
into God's promise of wisdom.

And maybe this is God
and Satan having tea
over Job, both concerned
he has suffered
too much blessing.

THE ANOINTING

I bumped the cup,
and a few drops of coffee
flopped over its lip
onto the title page
of Charles Bukowski's
Bone Palace Ballet.

After the reflex "Oh no!"
I thought: *Wait… it's Bukowski,*
poet of barstools, rats and roaches,
seedy motel rooms.

And I drink his words
like a poison that kills
slowly enough not to matter

and realize that coffee stains
in this book are nothing more,
yet nothing less, than a sprinkling
of Holy Water, a silent nod
to centuries of withheld blessings
for prostitutes and derelicts.

MY FOUR OF HEARTS

THE LINE.
    My heart holds love
    like the numb, burned hands
    of Hemingway's old man
    gripping the rope
    to the great fish
    that murders him at sea.

THE GAME.
    My heart is a chessboard,
    and I go through the motions
    of the last few moves—
    king one square to the right—
    before the opponent attaches
    "mate" to "check" and foregoes
    the final take in honor of the defeated.

THE STORM.
    My heart stands,
    a lone Monterey Cypress,
    thrashed and abused
    by a century of Decembers
    on the brooding California coast.

THE STATUE.
    My heart is the eye
    Lot's wife turns behind her,
    seeing the sulphuric fire,
    then looking down to watch
    the body turn to salt.

FOOTHOLD

I'd rather not believe my heart
is dead to love, having seen
one and one add up to three
or more, once or twice. But

there's a roaring silence
that my songs are given to.
It nails me now and then
to trees, whatever's handy.

Christ's hell was enough for all,
but I feel the need to follow
him there… on occasion…
to resurrect lost intentions.

Poetic as it may seem, it does nothing
to close the gaping chasm between
a potential friend and my self. But still,
the thought of a quiet toast over foam

and spray at sunset… tears mingling
with grapes… sustains my longing
for love unafraid of loss and separation,
letting its fields lie fallow for a time.

The seed is a simple thing—
miracle that it remains.
It is a faith in the harvest
I must find my way back to.

THE PRIVATE AND THE POET

Private First Class.
Morris—US Army.
Shaved head, full fatigues
and shin-high combat boots.
    He pokes away at a chrome
    Personal Digital Assistant
    atop a black leather planner,
    both full of what fuels him.

Two tables over, I sit—
greasy hair, 5 o'clock shadow,
frayed cargo shorts, Harvard
t-shirt, and black deck shoes.
    I peck away at a sketchbook
    with colored pens and whiteout.
    Wendell Berry's Collected Poems
    sit atop a paperback dictionary.

There was a time I would've shaken
my head at a young soldier's naïveté.
Now I see the foolishness was
altogether mine. And though
he may still shake his at me, I say—
God bless us both, the private…
and the poet. Our families, our dreams.

And save us from the pundit
and the president who tells him
who to kill and ignores the poet's
protests of such historically blind,
delusional and ungodly, commands.

124

BETWEEN TWO ARTISTS

Dear God,
            I have always admired
your work. And were it not for that,
I wouldn't bother you with this. But,

I must say that your installation piece
at the Point Lobos Nature Reserve
above Big Sur simply goes too far.

The Monterey pines are too tall,
the cypresses too fanned out in perfection
from trunks tied in intricate knots
that would take centuries
to unravel.
                        The cliffs appear
superimposed for dramatic effect
with impossible jags giving way
to fairytale caves that burst forth gushes
of blue water like a French soda topped
with a spray of whipped cream.

The crash of waves and explosions of foam
are too much like a Disney Land ride.
There are too many kinds of birds, too many
varieties of plants, and too much color
in both, I might add.

In short, it lacks integrity.
It does not speak to the truth
of the way things are. And I don't think
that viewers will trust, or believe,
its authenticity.

Too Much Information

I saw
God
tonight.

The More Things Change...

A tramp, a hussy, she'd be called,
if not for the recent wave
of political correctness.

She sits at a table with friends
on the coffee shop patio—

tousled, unwashed hair...
steely eyes of the street...
succulent, mud-brown limbs...

ember of cigarette flashing
across a small factory
of cheap silver jewelry.

A local gray-haired pastor
walking by on his way
back to church

steals a lengthy glance
at her tan breasts
heaving with laughter
and poetic license.

LOSIN' IT

God's gone mad.
   Of course,
how can you blame 'im?
Think about it...
you sink a few million—
or, ten thousand—years
[whichever you wanna believe]
into this creation project
and then, on the eighth day
your crowning achievement
sells itself down a shit river
of McDonalds and Wal-Marts.

We sent in a team of psychologists,
but he refused medication, laughing:

What the hell are you talking about?
I invented fucked-up. You know?
For color. But I never intended
for everyone *to hook up with it.*

We sent in a team of ministers,
but that *really* pissed 'im off.
Before they even got a chance
to whip out a tract and remind
the Lord of all Creation of his
Four Spiritual Laws, he shot off:

Look! I cut off communication
with you jackasses over 1800 years ago,
and I'm not about to start it back up again
with the black hole you've created,

sucking all the spiritual light
out of my universe.

We still see 'im now and then
among the rocks and trees…

walking the riverbank at night…
puffin' on a Swisher Sweet.

To My Surprise

It seems after a while
we'd give up any and all shock
at the human capacity
for mind-bending badness—

the holocaust, infanticide...
a mother pulling up in front
of Grandma's house one day,
with the new boyfriend,
and dropping the kids off,
permanently.

Then again, maybe that's the key
to the lock that evil hides
in its deep shadows:
                          Remain surprised.

Let the surges and jolts of war and rape
snap the buzzing wires of sensibility
like a May tornado in the plains.

Then jump up, if you can,
and stare the source in its face...
raise an arm with an extended forefinger...
and let the badness know
                          that you know.

Makes No Sense

Even with the invisible anvils
time has tied to my shoulders,
I smile more than I used to, raise
my head skyward and laugh.

Even with all the pennies lost
down the drain, the occasional
minor fortunes washed away
in a flood of bad decisions,
I'm more grateful than I used to be,
cherishing each minute awarded
like a quarter's-worth of time
on the mechanical horse in front
of the old grocery store.

Even though people are worse
than I had initially suspected
as a young man—full of crap
beyond imagination—I love them
more than ever, wanting to play
in their lives like a pony in the edges
of a pond, occasionally stopping
to take a long deep drink.

MAKEOVER

They've pulled him from the cross,
Brooks Brothered him out in a deep
navy suit with a maroon tie
and some nice leather Cole Haans.

When he tries to step into the synagogue
for prayer, they grab his elbow and suggest,
> *Uhh… we don't go there anymore. We have these*
> *nice new buildings out on the interstate. Much*
> *more conducive to larger P.A. systems, bigger*
> *offerings and live television feeds, you understand.*

He makes a dash for the tomb in hopes
of a few days rest, but they won't have it.
No time. Service starts at eleven hundred
hours, so hell will have to wait.

We're on air in five… and the techs
flip on the spotlights, blinding him
before he can raise his forearms in front
of his eyes, and only because he's God
does he understand the way in which
his image is beamed to a satellite
and then turned back towards earth
in a spray that reminds him of the
original rejection. He almost smiles
at this protestant stab at transubstantiation.

After the service—that leaves him
feeling unheard once again—

some of the wealthier members
want to take him to lunch
at the Oak Tree Country Club.

He would prefer a quiet hillside
for some meditation,
but they recommend Mondays
as being better for that and warn him
to watch his head as he ducks into
the back seat of the black stretch limo.

The pastor asks if he'd like to come over
and check out the Cowboys on FOX
or just head back to the Marriot for a nap.

And that's when Jesus breaks at a dead run
for the pond on the eighteenth hole
and wades out as far as he can,

because there is no boat this time…
because there are no fishermen
this time, and so he drops his face
into his hands, weeping uncontrollably.

Finding Jesus

First Baptist Church—my shoulders jerk up
when the new preacher's spit hits my cheek.

> *Folks! Jesus is comin' again!*
> *And it could be any minute now!*
> *Just look at the sins of this world!*

So, during the next tear-soaked prayer,
I slip out the back door to wait for him—
eyes scanning the sidewalks, I wonder
what he'll look like this time.

Impatience takes me across Webster St.
to the First Christian Church.
I look for him there. Nothin' doin'.

From there, I walk a block over
to University Blvd. and find no Savior
around McFarland Methodist either.

As a last ditch effort, I head south
on University to First Presbyterian
and catch my breath for a second
when I spot a homeless man
on a bench in the shade.
Not Him, but the closest thing
I've seen this morning. I ask
if he's seen any heavenly beings.
He raises a brown paper bag
and slobbers a profoundly quiet, "Yesss…"

He offers nothing more, so I shrug it off
and slide down a back alley to Campus Corner.
The Korean-owned Sunshine Store is open.
I buy a longneck and sink down
by the payphone out front.

Half way through the bottle, some guy
in camo pants and a sleeveless black T-shirt
squats down next to me. He asks for a sip.

Sure... I say, staring at the pavement.
He's respectfully quiet.

So, it's a minute or two
before I recognize him.

DEAD HERETICS SOCIETY

I've filled my home
    with sinners.

Frisbee players
    and Lutherans.

Gnostic engineers,
    Mormon environmentalists
    and a returned Baptist missionary...
        for color—more color
        than Zaccheus could have dreamed
        possible at his little party.

I've even thrown in
    a lawyer and a tax collector
    for biblical soundness.

They're all here for the poker
    and little smokies with a Bud.

All in preparation
    for the Savior's return.

YAP!

I'm afraid God may not be religious.

Matter of fact, the further I get
from religion's organized and fiery core,
the more the whole shebang looks like
a little angry dog yanking
on the pant leg of divinity...

divinity leaning over, speaking gently,
trying to help, but the little dog
doesn't understand divinity's language,

and so it just yelps and barks,
and it ain't ever gonna learn
to sit or heel. It just yaps
incessantly... because...

that's what little yappy dogs do.

Two Little Words

Apparently, we owe it to a baker somewhere,
in or around 1620, who put the words
"One" and "Way" together to label
a kind of bread eaten with oysters
before the meal... *One Way Bread.*

I'm curious what the ingredients were.
Because somewhere between the grating teeth
of the next few centuries, the words "one-way"
grew into two 3-headed dragons chained together,
spewing fire, and wreaking holy havoc.

These two little words set crazies like
Alexander Inglis and James Bryant Conant
off on a turn of the 20th Century warpath
thinking the straight-legged, knee-high boot-
stomping educational system of the Prussians
would be a good thing for our children;
make them better soldiers, floor-moppers,
and assembly-line workers—their heads
in a permanent bow to wealth.

These two words licensed the delusional alchemy
of the Southern Baptists, who infused the Holy Bible
with veins and arteries... gave it Frankenstein's heart
pumping with the blood of Dixie... then sewed on
the arms and legs of orthodoxy... and crammed
the brain of Judas into its skull—
a total eclipse of Christ.

And these two words make it impossible
for a president to admit his monstrous mistakes,
a secretary of defense to plead temporary insanity—
and for both to step back from the boiling cauldron
of far away nations, with the eyeballs and hands
of children floating in it—and admit
their heinous sins.

BAD

Sometimes
I just run out...
   out of steam...
and I tire of being good.
Because I'm just... well... tired.
I want to be bad. Good wears me out.

And nothing wears me out more than terminally
good people. Life bitch-slaps 'em into a smelly
dumpster full of rusty razor blades,
and they pop out bleeding
and praising Jesus.

I mean, even he appears
to have had his off moments.
People drove him nuts... while...
at the same time he loved them enough
to die for them. I recall a whip of ropes
and flying tables—one of the great
Gospel moments that helps me
believe in him even more...
because... we're all
thinkin' it—*Yeah!*
Give it to 'em, Jesus!
Those cheatin' bastards.

ELUSIVE

The center of the Milky Way's
swirl,   be   it
made of stars   or
c a r a m e l and white chocolate,
is the eye of my

                                          self

searching what lies just beyond
what is known

                                          for some new
candy   hidden
                    by God
in the lumpy folds of dark space,

                                          heaven's pantry.

141

ON THE WAY

Dad's retired and on his way
to pinch-hit preach in Tulsa
on an October Sunday morning.

He has a certain coffee stop
just before the turnpike,
a favorite form of meditation.

He pulls up to the window and
reaches for the football-shaped
rubber coin purse in his pocket

that I remember playing with
when I was five, or so.
She leans out, "Mornin'.

You all dressed up.
On your way to church?"
"Well, actually, I'm on my way

to Tulsa to preach this morning."
"Oh! So you a pastor." "Yes."
"Well... would you pray

for me right now? I got some
negative people and thoughts
in my life I needa get rid of."

Dad says sure, then she asks
for his hand. He reaches up.
He prays.   She squeezes.

And I imagine myself into
the car in line just behind him
seeing the white hand extended

from the cuff of a white shirt
clasped by the two beautiful
black hands at the ends of a gray

uniform and wonder if the sight
alone would be enough to bow
my head in worship with them.

REST FOR ANGELS

When I left Norman before sunrise
the temperature was in the mid-60s.
After sunset here in Manitou Springs,
I draw in the stiff elixir of 31 degrees.

Once again, I am in the one-seater booth
in the back corner of the Twelve Tribe's—
    a Hobbit hole of a coffee shop—
reading and writing poetry
under a dangling yellow bulb.

And once again, I feel my breath
slow down... just behind
the bridge of my nose.

And I know the hard-working angels
who were assigned to hold together
my cracked and fractured mind—
    to administer my daily doses
    of grace and pardon—

have sat down by the chilly springs
just out the wood-paned window
to finally rest and talk
about other things
for a while.

VERB PLAY

When I'm forced to spend time around zealous minister types, I keep hearing about the necessity of reaching out to the "unchurched." The obvious implication being: we need to "church" the "unchurched."

Now, this particular verbish usage of the word "unchurch" does not appear in my fairly large dictionary. What I do see, however, is the transitive verb that means to excommunicate. This definition is clearer to me. And it helps me organize my response:

Dear friends,

Our deepest need is not to "church" the "unchurched," but to "dechurch" the "enchurched"—that is to say, the excessively "churched."

God Save Me from Your Followers

has ceased to be a humorous bumper sticker. It is now a genuine fear for many of the "unchurched" to which you refer.

And as we look for solutions, a good place to start would be to "depolitic" "enchurched" leaders. But, in the end, [and while we're in the practice of verbing up nouns] nothing—and I reiterate... nothing—supersedes the desperate need for Christians to "reJesus" the church.

CULMINATION OF THE SPECIES

He has a stuffed baboon holding an open copy of Darwin's *Origin of the Species* as if it's reading it. It sits on a table in his office at the seminary. He is the president. Apparently, he is quite the big game hunter. First-hand accounts—friends who have actually gone on safari in said office—tell of a veritable carnival of trophies from leopards and lions to sundry species of deer... even a legless giraffe lounging peacefully on the floor.

The story is that a group of seminary daycare children were touring the office one day. As would be expected, more than a few uncertain, if not terrified, sets of little eyes were glued to the giraffe— as if all the other animals wouldn't be horrifying enough. With its head towering up to the ceiling, the president offered these words of comfort to the kids: *Giraffes only live to be about 35, and this one was about 34. So it would have died soon.*

The fabulous tail to this tale is that one of the children then asked: *How old are you mister?*

Children often leave us with little need to sum things up. And whether the story is true or not, the office, the death it contains, and the man presiding over it *are* true. And so, I'm beginning to believe the Southern Baptists are correct in their vehement denial of the Theory of Evolution. And this man may very well be the best piece of evidence.

A FAITH BETWEEN

I'm trying to decide what I believe in
anymore. And I begin with consideration
of what I don't believe in anymore:

I don't believe in hell anymore, like it's
some sort of Club Dead on the coast
of Baja California, where the hot tubs

boil instead of bubble, and the ocean
breaks with waves of molten lava...
or where long massages are given

with pumice stones, and boiling cocktails
of liquid silver—with little lead umbrellas—
come with an hors d' oeuvre of live sand crabs.

And if I still believe in some heaven,
it is in the sense that I'm certain
I have been there without dying...

meaning, I think it's open for business,
but we've lost the map and don't wanna
drive over to the other side to look for it

anymore. It's just that my ex-wife called
a few minutes ago... and they've taken
a look at the x-rays... and they're afraid

my little girl's got pneumonia. And so,
I'm rummaging through my backpack
because there's something I've lost,
and I really, really need to find it.

SUNDAY SCHOOL

Cain swoops in to Sunday school
on the wings of pterodactyls...

a virginal sip of blood and murder
for wide-eyed first grade Abels.

In Fusion

I'm beginning to understand
why so many older people are quiet
in the mix of family and social gatherings,
the back row in big church, or the picnic
that follows. What I once thought was
a lack of liveliness, I now see as patience.

They softly suffer through our absolutes,
truths we're so sure are roasted to perfection.

They listen to the college punk in the pulpit
and smile at an ignorance they survived,
remembering how it burned in flames of failure.

And I, a teacher between generations,
field questions of "What's it all about?"
and have only learned enough to point
to the back where seasoned lips wait
to speak what tender ears can't yet hear.

And I stand there in the middle,
stretching for a hand of each,
hoping I won't blow
like a low amp fuse
in the surge of power
when the circuit completes.

LONG LAY THE WORLD

I perform a few songs and carols
in the midnight Christmas Eve service
every year at my dad's church.
Don't think I've missed in a decade.

It's a soft hour. Yet, I've somehow managed
to turn it into work. Religion's desperation
rakes fingernails across the letters of scripture
on the chalkboard to the point I've lost all focus.

But in the back hallway, retuning my guitar
between songs, I see a police car blaze by
on Main. Guns and knives don't take holidays.
I feel a metaphor slice into my sagging heart.

I go back out to close with O Holy Night,
to look like my mind's on manger scenes,
and instead, pray a silent prayer of peace
for the endless work of uniforms and badges.

BOUND FOR PARADISE

Who else does that...
just declares
a "Day of Rage?"

Now... dadgummit... I am
a flaming liberal-hippie-type,
and I'm supposed to love everyone—

except maybe CEOs and senators.
I'm supposed to sympathize
with the Palestinian cause. Then

they go and actually set aside
a day devoted to hate and rage.
That's all they're going to do...

outside of maybe some dinner
around eight or nine o'clock.
They're going to "Rage" against Jews

and Israelis, and American capitalist dogs,
oh, and don't forget those damn British
who snuck off in '48 and left them in this mess.

Now... the Jews have the "Days of Awe,"
and Daytona has its "Days of Thunder."
But this... this legacy to grandchildren?

Yes Punkin, those were the days...
The Days of Rage... when we poured
into the streets... and hated people.

HALF

In dreams of hope and blood,
I place a rusty bucket below
my soul's leaky faucet... something
to catch the drip of words
that wage attrition's war
on my mind.

Sometimes, when it looks half empty,
I throw it out the back door,
believing it will nourish beauty...
art of a more wordless nature.

Other times, when it appears half full,
I dash it onto a canvas, stand over it
for hours, days... my head
cocked to the right...
then to the left...

believing that even half
of all this crazy world's
hopeful and bloody dreams
could, somehow,
mean the difference.

Hobson's Choice

2002

Poetry is what happens when nothing else can.

~ Charles Bukowski

On the Introduction
to *Hobson's Choice*

Hopeful cynic.

These two words comprised the entire opening paragraph of the introduction to *Hobson's Choice*—an introduction that I pulled from the radioactive residue of the introduction to my master's thesis. I considered it my best shot at a self-description. I then went on to explain it. That was a mistake... as was the rest of the 20 or so pages of the introduction to that book. So, since that's the only paragraph I still agree with, I'll not excerpt any more from it.

I maintain the painful truth that the best piece of writing in my first book was the preface that Billy Crockett had so kindly written for me. That's why I included it, word for word, in this new book that does its best to fix up old things...

—Nathan

A book of poetry is not a travelogue. They have another section in the store for that. It is a crisis. Poetry is a precarious high-wire act of faith in words to reveal, to name, to remember, to whisper or shout the news of who we are, again and again. It is as necessary an item as is liable to be on any shelf in any store, with the possible exception of diapers and the blues. The foreknowledge of the dim state of poetry sales must be particularly liberating to the author. He may apply himself single-mindedly to the crisis at hand.

Nathan Brown's poems are experiments in soul-play. His keen eye for the hidden agendas of this world is tempered with a wink and the suspicion of joy. This collection of poems has suggested to me the idea of the poet-sleuth. See him there with one giant eye behind the thick rounded glass. He is always looking. Time may stretch out forever in the discovery of a certain "softness" or a slight catch in the breath. And that's not a problem because the poet's currency is time. It's not that he has any more of it than anybody else – he's simply chosen to spend it investigating the interiors and intimations of his world. He is always willing to see what he sees. Willing to give up the idea of "horseness" for the possibility of an actual horse, whatever that may be.

So who was Hobson anyway, and what was his dilemma? Turns out Hobson himself had no particular choice to make. An Englishman who leased horses to travelers, Hobson was famous for requiring his clients to take the horse nearest the door, whatever the condition. The phrase "Hobson's choice" has come to mean, therefore, a "seeming" choice where, in fact, there is no choice at all. I "chose" to drive the beat-up powder blue station wagon with the plywood back seat my granddad bought at a government auction. As a college student with little income, what were my options? One thinks also of the plight of the American Indians "negotiating" for a life on the reservation. You take what you are handed.

So the irony is rich in the author's title. Bearing the inheritance of racial and economic privilege, he seems to enjoy a world of options. He may choose his career, his friends, his vacations, his schooling, his entertainment, his passion. He is only denied one thing – credibility. What a strange and silent barricade surrounds the poet from among the envied majority. He is given art schools and English degrees but no authorization to use his voice in the community. He has no right to speak according to prevailing sentiment. He has not earned it. He can take the lame horse closest to the door.

So what constitutes literary authority? All have experienced the glib misuse of language by those who don words like Easter bonnets – decoration for effect. Sarcasm, sentimentality, and lies pervade our culture from ad copy to the Sunday sermon. It is no surprise when language is employed to cover-up motivations rather than reveal. Liza Doolittle's response nails it: "Words, words, words - nothing but words!"

What gives words significance? What gives them the capacity, the passenger space, to carry the reader to a place of meaning? It would seem to require a certain seed-like connection to experience. Life begets words. Some have posted their suffering on wailing walls and federal buildings with profound healing effect, to the shame of those who co-opt these words for commercial and political gain.

So who is entitled to write? Only those who live through great oppression and suffering? Only those who have been handed-off, ignored, mistreated and forgotten in the world? Certainly the community must hear from its unremembered self. But what about the voice of the middle class white heterosexual adult male who's never been to jail and does not find himself victimized, profiled or ushered into a symbolic role for the emergence of a minority power base?

There is no existential privilege for any of us. We are all given as a sentence and a birthright the task of making meaning of our short walk on this planet and our perfectly sure demise. In this we have equality. In this I am a brother to kings, serfs, and holocaust victims. All of our ears ring with the dizzy spells belonging to every human inhabitant of this spinning mother-ball in the Milky Way somewhere on its way to somewhere.

The authority to express derives simply from the capacity to feel one's way along this world, to take notes, and to risk posting the results. And one more thing – one must love words when they do, sometimes, integrate and illuminate experience.

So, what is the poet's choice? Maybe it is simply whether to show up. He sees the crisis. He knows he must employ language. He must redeem words. So, it is finally a question of loyalty. He is credible, he is authorized, because he knows he is in the world for this – to name the animals, to respond, to provoke, to conflict, to defend, to risk, to honor. It is a vital calling, not only to society's marginalized, but to each rare and courageous self of any age, color, creed and bank balance, willing to take up the life as well as the pen.

—Billy Crockett
November 1, 2001

3 QUARTERS

she didn't look to have a dime
to her brown   scarf   name

but she must have had
at least a couple
of crumpled up dollars
left over
from the welfare check

she bought the breakfast special—
scrambled eggs n' pancakes

after tax
she got 3 quarters back

with those she played
the jukebox—

Rosemary Clooney
    got the feet tappin'

The Beatles
    cracked a smile

n' Ol' Blue Eyes
    made us both cry

BLACK STUFF

they look
happy.
he's older, grayer
in a black shirt n' jeans.
she's younger, blonder
in a black shirt n' jeans.

he talks on a black cell phone
pulled from a black briefcase.

she writes in a notebook
pulled from a black bag.

he's on hold, so he talks to her
about bills n' credit cards
n' operating in the black.

he talks about interest
on her account.

they kiss n' talk
about a white wedding.

they look
in separate directions
n' wonder

who'll get all the black stuff
if it doesn't work out.

DENIED SPACE

A dry wind blows

on civilization

```
  —       —
|   NO    |
| PARKING |
  —       —
```

signs

jerk in the gusts...

a rattling anthem

EVERY DAY   EVERY TIME

art dies   every day   every time

       Mozart   repeats on the radio

art dies   every day   every time

       Monet   becomes a postcard

art dies   every day   every time

       Rodin   is reduced to plastic

art dies   every day   every time

       Shakespeare   is slapped on celluloid

art dies…

HOMELESS

They sit by the nighttime blue
of Honolulu's sea...
a bench   on the boardwalk
of pacific Waikiki...
laughingly inhaling
familiar brackish air   strangely
sardonically happy.

> Across the street
> through the windows
> of a second   story   ballroom
> the dull yellow of crystal chandeliers
> barely reveals the red and white helium
> bubbles   tied to the backs of chairs.

Maybe the couple is secretly laughing
at those poor bastards up there
in their cumbersome clothes
of black and white pomp
and dreadful ceremony

dancing to a third-rate cover band
that can't seem to drum up
their favorite tune.

LAS VEGAS

Pair o' dice

Lost

PURCHASE

I pop into Target
on a painfully muggy afternoon—
one of those must-do purchases
I never want to take time for.

I'm lost as I roam the renovated aisles.
nothing is where it had been
    when I bought my orange skate-board
        23 years ago.

At the bright red counter
I thoughtfully spill blue n' yellow items
    —a spray-can of WD-40
        Household n' Automotive Lubricant
    —Preparation H® Hemorrhoidal Suppositories.

Avoiding the pitying posture and gaze
of the chirpy-eyed, sigmoidally sound sales clerk,
the epiphanal thought suffuses my mind—

    "One way 'r another, baby...

        one   way   or   another..."

SHE TRIES

she tries so hard to fill

s p a c e s   left

by a
          psychotically religious   mother
and a
          religiously psychotic   father

she tries sO *H*arrrrd

     to smoo**t**h   out th*E* rough p*L*aces

                              in her *P*last

allforthehopeofalittlecontinuity

something
               someone
                         she can count on

but
          walls…
                    the walls…

SUBURBA PASTORA

You're next!
Oh verdant field of my childhood.

You are next,
Oh remnant of the once Great Plains,
Home of the fiery cardinal.

My tears wet your sandy belly,
Pregnant with concrete and brick.

You are next,
Oh friend of better days.
You're next...

THE MAUL

the hook sets
deep in the throat
of the need to possess

silver n' gold
lusty shine
deadly grip
hand   stuck in the jar

sticky walls
plastic motel
a flutter of limbs
the final throes

people of fashion,
taste and intelligence
haul it all back to the cell
hang it   store it
        ∿ the fish flips back in the sea ∿
hide it   hoard it
        ∿ the monkey n' cockroach run free ∿

To – From

Noiseragingnewsblaringhornshonkingdogsbarkingkid
sscreamingbabiescryingdrillsdrillingjetsroaringdrivers
yellingsirenswailingradiosblastingspeakersthumpingtir
esscreechingalarmsringingenginesru m b l i n g f a n s
h u m m i n g w a t e r d r i p p i n g c l o c k s
t i c k i n g c r i c k e t s c h i r p i n g
b r e e z e s w h i s p e r i n g

wilderness

silence

revelation

wisdom

w h i s p e r i n g b r e e z e s
c h i r p i n g c r i c k e t s t i c k i n g
c l o c k s d r i p p i n g w a t e r h u m m i n g
fansrumblingenginesringingalarmsscreechingtiresthu
mpingspeakersblastingradioswailingsirensyellingdrive
rsroaringjetsdrillingdrillscryingbabiesscreamingkidsba
rkingdogshonkinghornsblaringnewsragingnoise

TRAVELER

A jacket
on a broomstick
slumped in another
useless heap
in a foreign
border town.

He only wants
to get back home,
but he's currently
misunderstood
in three different
languages.

The villagers
would pay his way
just to get rid of him,
but they don't have
the money either.

Maybe they
were on their way
somewhere
one time
too.

Yet under an Angel's unseen tutelage
the outcast child, enchanted by the sun,
will recognize in all he eats and drinks
golden ambrosia and nectar of the gods.

With winds for playmate and with clouds for nurse,
he sings the very stations of his cross –
the Spirit who attends his pilgrimage
weeps to see him happy as a bird.

—Charles Baudelaire
Les Fleurs du Mal

BAUDELAIRE'S ANGEL

Oh God, send Baudelaire's angel
to the blameless side of my little girl
to walk with her in the soundless moments
in between
and whisper love in life and art
in spite of clamoring influences.

Oh God, send Baudelaire's angel
to shepherd her increasing days
that she might someday relish
the taste of ambrosia
and raise a stem of nectar to the heavens
in a silent nod to the other truth.

FLYING

Another flying dream.

I've had them all my life,
but this time
my baby girl flew too.

At first, my heart
pounded with fear
at that increased rate
that prunes a parent's years.

But I soon realized
she was fine.

She swirled and turned
in graceful arcs among stars,
then softly came to rest
in my anxious arms.

But only for a while.

On waking, I understood
all the useless no's.

HER WORLD

Purple elephants
Sway in blue fields
Of canary grass.

Green whales
Sound in pink oceans
Under a yellow sky.

White birds
Sit in orange trees
With copper trunks
And silver fruit.

BABY BUMPY

Baby Bumpy
Is getting all thumpy
N' banging around inside of her mummy

She's getting all jumpy
N' wiggling her rumpy
N' stretching out mummy's poor little tummy

But lately she's grumpy
N' down in a slumpy
Cause the food in mummy's tummy's not yummy

It's way too lumpy
Clotted n' clumpy
It's time for some womb service that isn't so crummy!

So Daddy Dumpy
Best get off his humpy
Instead of sittin' there actin' all chummy

Cause mummy's tummy's not yummy, it's crummy
Now, go get some good food you great big ol' dummy!

THE LUCKY SOCK

I was the lucky sock today
Who from the dryer snuck away

Never again to have to eat
My owner's smelly, sweaty feet

I hid behind the detergent box
With all the other single socks

Hoping I'd be safe back there
Until he bought a brand new pair

A few days later, I froze at the sound
The box was moving, I knew I was found

He saw me, grabbed me 'n started to shout
He acted all crazy 'n waved me about

"I don't believe it!" I heard him say
"I JUST threw your matching sock away!"

ALIYA

In the belly of a Boeing whale,
having waited all their lives,
they wait for the mouth to y a w n.

Squinting eyes
meet a Mediterranean blaze.
Burning nostrils
relish turbine fumes
foreshadowing Judean winds.

Canvas bags
and wobbling canes
stream down Jacob's Ladder
to embrace again
Canaan's fiery shores.

Tears soak oily pavement
sprouting grace through cracks.
Noah's dormant rainbow returns
with a long forgotten promise.

Clasped hands
uplifted eyes
cry—

"Ha Aretz Yisrael!

    I am home…"

All Hayell!

All hail! The Southern Baptist Convention
O blessed brotherhood of rectal retention

A Christian majority   A moral coalition
A liberal purging   of all moderation

We tirelessly seek   defemination
And by our behavior   disprove evolution

"They'll know we are Christians by our litigations
By our love   and literal   interpretations"

"By devout duress we'll amass congregations
Consuming the lost in mass conflagrations"

"Then up from the ashes will rise exclamations
Uplifted glasses   divine salutations—

To original texts!   and infallibation!
All hayell! The Southern Baptist Convention!"

JERICHO

it
  is
a long
and bumpy
road   down
through terra cotta
mountains   past
goat skin tents   with
TV antennas n' a pepto-
pink Mercedes   its wheels
                    to the sky

hundreds of feet   below sea level
air so thick it does the breathing for me
burning   ripping at the open windows
sanding down my face tugging at my hair

my shirt is soaked   stuck to the seat-back
                    my right arm sunburned

the town is shut down   orders of the PLO a
floundering demonstration   eons of frustration
Yassir Are ya' fat and getting old? Ah hell, I'll have
                    a piece o' that prize too

a favorite little restaurant meaningfully blown to bits

by anger beaming down from a merciless Judean sun

JOHN THE SOUTHERN BAPTIST

I slip into the hallway

  behind the sanctuary,

    when suddenly   a voice

                                  calling

scripture,   out

from little white speakers   in the

ceiling—mounted,

    bounces off

    brick walls painted   desert—

    white—

                               "Repent!"

echoes   -es   -es

coming to rest

in the mottled blue carpet.   "Repent!"

MAY DAY
Saturday – May 1, 1999

black Nike Airs set a quick pace
untanned calves flash in the sunlight
a saffron robe with brown tasseled belt
    flaps down the side of I-35

wire-frame glasses struggle to support
    a concerned cro-magnon brow
brown bushy hair tries
    to cover the shiny cue ball

a stoic shoulder
    harnessed with a nine foot cross—
        black rubber wheel attached to the bottom—
            Wal-Mart special

a sign on the back of the cross
roars at traffic coming up behind:

        GOD WANTS
        PRAYER
        BACK IN
        SCHOOL

and I'm thinkin'—

                        Jesus didn't get a wheel

SOUTHERN-FRIED-SUNDAYS

Mine was a
Sunday-after-church-fried-chicken-childhood.
Cornbread-n'-squash-casserole-afternoons gave way
to mandarin-orange-Jello-salad-sunsets.
Sweet-potato-evenings by roasted-marshmallow-fires
always left time for devil'd-egg-stories
n' home-made-ice-cream-tunes.
Guitars were the nuts n' chocolate sauce
of unenforced bed times.

It was a mythical age when fam'lies stuck together
like day-old-steamed-white-rice. And laughter
was as simple as a tipped-over-lawn-chair
    and ashes on the end of a burnt hot dog.

Baptists'll tell ya' *"church* is ever'thing."
But they all know without saying—
God is in the good food
and licked fingers
of a Sunday after
noon.

THE WAILING WALL

I hear the wall wailing
from the weight of our prayers
that eternally prick its millennial cracks

I hear the wall wailing
from the ageless torment
of war and destruction and unending tears

It cries to the east,
"blind-hinged hatred has abandoned your souls"

It cries to the west,
"the sleep of complacency has hooded your eyes"

I hear the wall wailing
it cries to me now,
"embrace the blood of my murdered children"

I hear
        the wall
                wailing

COFFEE

I just drank coffee.

I never drink coffee.

It's a reception for academiacs.

I suppose the coffee, maybe
makes me feel more academic,

or at least ephemerally endemic.

Anyway,

they others're all drinking it,
and they seem to know a lot of stuff.

Compound Spiral

…dry run   . ……….dry

down town   .   run down

hall way   .   town hall

faring well   .   way faring

water snake   .   well water

oil lamp   .   snake oil

shade tree   .   lamp shade

house guest   .   tree house

bed room   .   guest bed

service man   .   room service

power play   .   man power

back bone   .   play back

dry……….   .   bone dry…

185

HOBSON'S CHOICE

I SIT
a w h i t e a m e r i c a n m a l e
in my little Barnes & Noble Bookstore
b i b l e b e l t b u c k l e m i d d l e c l a s s
with my little pen and pad
c a r h o u s e d o g k i d w i f e
and try to birth a golden language.

I FEAR
w o r k 8 h o u r d a y s w e e k e n d s o f f
however   –   I have
p a r e n t s s t i l l m a r r i e d a n d h a p p y
no axe-wielding trial
    worthy of CNN
no dripping childhood wound
    from which to muster miserable images
no inherited holocaust
    raging me to remembrance

I HAVE
f o o d c l o t h e s t v h o t c h o c o l a t e
    lost no child
    fought no war
    committed no crime

NO LICENSE
to write

My Question to Freud

So, what is it that forces that index finger
   on my right hand
to reach over and incessantly pick the cuticle
   of my left hand's middle finger
      during class?

Was it the time my parents left me
   at the neighbors when I was four?
Was it the first time I saw my mother cry?
Was it the time...

Or is it that floating baboon gene
   carefully honed by evolution
      in response to centuries
         of boredom?

ORPHEUS SING!

Orpheus sing!
      Sing on, my brother—
      drawing tears
      from Hell's betrothed.

Orpheus sing!
      Sing on, my brother—
      though you look back
      and lose her forever.

Sing!
      Sing on, my brother.

RHETORIC

after all of the words
the nouns and the verbs
I froze in a moment of dread

for   what seemed to be something
turned out to be nothing
no thing had actually been said

so   I hope in some way
somehow, someday
before the rolls are read

to think of a new thing
and *some*day say *some*thing
for nothing's already been said

SOMETHING

There I was
applauding

                something

I didn't understand,
but
it must have meant

                something

because
there were people
with glasses,
gray hair,
and sleek pens
writing

                some things

They were laughing
It must've been a

                fun thing

So I leaned forward
looking
as if I were listening,
hands clasped
beneath my chin
thinking

                something

THE VILLAINOUS NELLE

I held in contempt, yet admired as well
With utmost respect, I secretly hated
The one who created the villainous nelle

The recurring lines, the tenth syllabelle
Impossible rhymes and meters upended
I held in contempt, yet admired as well

Its difficult structure, Gematraic helle
In doing my best, I wriggled and wrested
With the one who created the villainous nelle

Plenty of paper, ink's bottomless welle
A poet with plenty of time to be wasted
I held in contempt, yet admired as well

The lack of TV was easy to telle
In the poetic home of the one whom I hated
The one who created the villainous nelle

They have now padded my artistic celle
From when I combated, cried then decided
I held in contempt, yet admired as welle
The one who created the villainous nelle

AH, THANKSGIVING

That wonderful time of year
when we cut up and roast

all the turkeys in the family
into scrutinized pieces

when brief moments find us
paired off in bedrooms and bathrooms

BEN YEHUDA STREET

thick gray fur
appears on the porch
of the back alley café

      her
            tail
                 moves
             slowly
         back
         and
           forth

warm chair
by the table
recently vacated
of ice cream groupies

now onto the table
         chocolate?   no.
         strawberry?   no.
ahhh…   vanilla.

      her
            tail
                 moves
             slowly
         back
         and
           forth

THE COOL WINDS CAME

the cool winds came
for the third time this spring
the heat crept backwards
and sat on its haunches

I think I felt Atlas's shoulders relax
and the soul
of the dwellers
sigh

GREEN LADY

It was that "green lady" on Star Trek
who ravaged my budding hormones.
Don't remember a plot.
Just that twitching, salty dance.　　But

it wasn't gyration or bulging shapes
or eyes like eggs in salad…
…maybe the blazing white of teeth
…or the flash of pink in the tongue.

But absolutely—

it was that smooth green skin
like a peeled avocado
I knew would slip between fingers
and smell of mint, sage, or seawater.

I felt my confused body stir.
I burned to know the forbidden:
Does the green reach up inside
beneath those barely clothes?

NIGHT GAME

Maybe it's those lights
holding on to Joshua's sun
and fans dressed against the cold
like dutiful soldiers
wiggling toes and fingers
to keep a flow of blood
while hunkered in the hole.

Or maybe it's that stadium hotdog
you have to take your gloves off to eat,
its warmth bypassing concerns
of animal by-products.
You gotta lick the ketchup
and mustard off fingers,
cause there ain't no way
you're gonna stick 'em under
that ice cold tap
in the men's urinal barn,
never to feel them again.

Maybe it's the way
you hold that cup of hot chocolate
between both hands,
a sacred drink offering
raised to angry sport gods
in hopes your team won't
get its ass kicked this time.
Of course,
the cup takes a pit stop
at chapped but grateful lips
on the way up.

Or maybe
it's about believing—
that never-ending hope
that somehow,
some way,
even though you're 3 and 8
for the season,
fate, taking a night off,
will crinkle a corner of its mouth
and your team will win.

PERCEPTION

is it merely a pat of soft butter,
or the crowning of life's next moment?

is it a sliced cinnamon-raisin bagel,
or the glory of daily ceremony?

is it a musty, rough-hewn table
  a squeaking chair
    a mottled steel knife
      and a filmy wood-frame window,
or   space   engorged with meaning
  fraught with motionless desire?

are they merely evening rays,
or divine hands stretching?

SUNSET SYMPHONY

. . . .

. . . .

. . . .

the clouds are settling

into their places

the breeze is tuning

up   to middle sea

. . . . . .

. . . .

and the sun is dimming the lights

. . . .

. . . . . .

the curtain raises

and gilded rays

shoot across the sky

a path of golden light

leaps across the water

as sand and surf

roar with applause

. . . .

. . .

WORDLESS

I'm on one of those walks—
　　one of those too-much-sodium
　　　　cholesterol-stress-you're-dying walks.

My body warms
　　to the falling orange of the horizon
　　　　and the pace of my feet.

My Reeboks scratch the sidewalk
　　as a bass breaks the surface
　　　　of the wind-rippled pond.

And I stop dead in my tracks
　　when, jutting from the end
　　　　of a leafless branch,

the silhouette of the Great Blue Heron
　　turns its head,
　　　　beak pointing

straight at my cranium…
　　beaming a wordless message
　　　　directly　into　my　soul…

something along the lines of

　　　　s l o w　d o w　n

Nathan Brown is a musician, photographer, and award-winning poet from Norman, Oklahoma. He holds a PhD in *Creative and Professional Writing* from the University of Oklahoma and teaches there as well. Mostly he travels now, though, performing readings and concerts as well as speaking and leading workshops in high schools, universities, and community organizations on creativity, creative writing, and the need for readers to not give up on poetry.

He has published seven previous books: *Letters to the One-Armed Poet: A Memoir of Friendship, Loss, and Butternut Squash Ravioli* (2011), *My Sideways Heart* (2010), *Two Tables Over* (2008)—Winner of the 2009 Oklahoma Book Award, *Not Exactly Job* (2007)—a finalist for the Oklahoma Book Award, *Ashes Over the Southwest* (2005), *Suffer the Little Voices* (2005)—a finalist for the Oklahoma Book Award, and *Hobson's Choice* (2002). He is also the co-editor, along with his wife, Ashley, of *AGAVE: A Celebration of Tequila in Story, Song, Poetry, Essay, and Graphic Art.*

His poem, "Little Jerusalems," was recently nominated for the Pushcart Prize. And in 2010, he released an album of all-original songs, *Gypsy Moon.*

Nathan's work has appeared in: *World Literature Today; Concho River Review; Blue Rock Review; Descant; Texas Poetry Calendar; Sugar Mule; Di-verse-city* (anthology of the *Austin International Poetry Festival*); *Wichita Falls Literature and Art Review;* "Walt's Corner" of *The Long-Islander* newspaper (a column started by Whitman in 1838); *Langdon Review of the Arts in Texas; Oklahoma Today Magazine; Oklahoma Humanities Magazine; Blood and Thunder; Blueberry Rain and Chocolate Snow; Windhover; Byline Magazine; Blue Hole:*

Magazine of the Georgetown Poetry Festival; Christian Ethics Today; Crosstimbers; and *Poetrybay.com*... as well as in five anthologies: *Travelin' Music: A Poetic Tribute to Woody Guthrie* (Village Books Press, Cheyenne), *Two Southwests* (VAC, Chicago), *Ain't Nobody That Can Sing Like Me: New Oklahoma Writing* (Mongrel Empire Press, Albuquerque), *Wingbeats: Exercises & Practice in Poetry* (Dos Gatos Press, Austin), *New Poetry Appreciation* (Yunnan University Press, Kunming, China).

For more info, and to order books, go to:

brownlines.com

...Photo by Rodney Bursiel

CPSIA information can be obtained at www.ICGtesting.com
Printed in the USA
LVOW080422160312

273218LV00001B/6/P